Guide to Cheeses
of the World

Choosing, recognizing, tasting
1200 cheeses from around the world

Despite all the care and attention taken in compiling this book, and taking account of the extensive fluctuation in the regulations, practices and usage in this field, the authors and the publisher cannot consider themselves directly or indirectly responsible for errors, omissions or information contained in this work. It is explicitly stated that the objective of this book is to provide a clear and practical guide for the use of consumers; it is not a reference book aimed at specialists in the subject.

The photographs used to illustrate this work were taken by Jacques Guillard. The photographs accompanying the 'favourites' notes were taken by Daniel Czap.

The text for the book was derived from *Fromages du Monde*, by Roland Barthélemy and Arnaud Sperat-Czar, published by Hachette Pratique.

Management: Stephen Bateman and Pierre-Jean Furet
Editorial Manager: Brigitte Éveno
Edited by: Catherine Donzel and Charlotte Buch-Muller
Cover: Nicole Dassonville
Cover photograph: Pierre Desgrieux (Sucré salé)
Layout: François Lemaire
Make-up: Marie Vendittelli (Looping)
Production: Claire Leleu

First published by Hachette Livre
43 Quai de Grenelle, Paris 75905, Cedex 15, France
Under the title *Guide du Fromage*
© 2003, Hachette Livre
All rights reserved

English language translation produced by Translate-A-Book, Oxford

This edition published by Hachette Illustrated UK, Octopus Publishing Group, 2-4 Heron Quays, London, E14 4JP
English Translation © 2005, Octopus Publishing Group Ltd, London

Printed by Toppan Printing Co., (HK) Ltd.

ISBN 10: 1 84430 151 6
ISBN 13: 978 1 84430 151 5

Guide to Cheeses
of the World

Choosing, recognizing, tasting
1200 cheeses from around the world

ROLAND BARTHÉLEMY AND ARNAUD SPERAT-CZAR

Photographs: Daniel Czap
Jacques Guillard

HACHETTE
Illustrated

Here at last is a guide that will answer all the questions cheese-lovers ask themselves about buying and eating cheese and savouring it to its best advantage. This book will show you how to avoid the pitfalls and reveals a host of tricks of the trade that will allow you to enjoy your favourite cheeses to the full. How to produce a varied cheese-board? What wine to serve with Beaufort, Roquefort, or goat's milk cheeses? Does cheese really pile on the pounds? These are some examples of the practical advice on choosing, keeping, serving and eating cheeses offered by this guide. Let yourself be led on to discover the 1,200 or so cheeses from around the world, classified by the authors according to cheese 'families'. Clear and comprehensive entries allow you to see at a glance the principal characteristics of any product: country of origin, *terroir* (region), type of milk (cow's, ewe's, goat's), label, optimum period of *affinage* (ripening) etc. Throughout the pages to come, Roland Barthélemy, highly reputed Parisian cheese retailer and *affineur*, will share with you his hundred favourite cheeses, set out in detailed, illustrated entries packed with anecdotes about cheese-making.

His star cheeses will no longer hold any secrets for you. The richness of the illustrations lets you visualize the main cheeses and learn to recognize them. An index at the end of the book makes for quick and efficient research. Also included is a glossary of the most frequently used terms in the cheese world. Happy tasting!

ALL ABOUT CHEESE

1200 CHEESES, 100 FAVOURITES

APPENDIX

All about
cheese

FROM MILK TO CHEESE: THE MINIMUM YOU NEED TO KNOW

The result of a combination of practical experience and scientific fact, cheese making rests on an unchanging sequence of events: all cheese is milk that has been coagulated, drained to a greater or lesser degree and, if necessary, ripened.

The milk is often partially skimmed (traditionally the cream is made into butter). In principle, full-cream milk produces a more supple curd. Raw milk has the maximum potential for flavour; milk that has undergone full or partial pasteurization will generally give a more standardized product. The by-products of milk – whey and buttermilk – contain residual proteins and can also be made into cheese. Coagulation is the process that causes milk proteins to link together. It happens spontaneously when milk is left at an ambient temperature: its own ferments and the bacteria present in the atmosphere cause it to 'turn' and curdle. To help the process the cheese-maker may add other milk ferments (essential when the milk is of poor quality or has been pasteurized) or microbiological coagulant enzymes, or even natural rennet taken from the stomachs of young calves. For the most part, curd made using predominantly lactic ferments makes cheeses that harden and dry as they mature (this applies to most goat's milk cheeses), while curd made mainly with rennet (also called 'soft curd') is better for softer textures, such as Brie or Munster.

The curd, once it is put into moulds (to give it the desired shape), must be drained of its liquids, to a greater or lesser degree according to the result required: the less moisture it retains, the longer it will keep. Drainage can be slow and spontaneous or accelerated by chopping, crumbling or pressing the curd, or even heating it to around 50°C (120°F).

Cheeses are ripened by the action of different micro-organisms, such as bacteria, moulds or yeasts, which work either on the surface or within the curd. The rind forms, aided by salt, the curd is transformed and the flavour asserts itself.

Making farmhouse Gaperon, at Montgaçon.

CHEESES THROUGH THE SEASONS: THE BEST OF SPRING

Spring is by far the best season for most cheeses. Here are a few tips to help you get the most out of this period of plenty.

Goat's milk cheeses return with a flourish. Their short ripening period (ten days to one month) makes them quickly available on the market. They arrive from central France (Saint-Maure-de-Touraine, Selle-sur-Cher, Crottin de Chavignol), from Poitou-Charentes (Chabichou), the Rhône-Alpes region (Brique du Forez, Chevrotin, Persillé des Aravis), from the south of the Massif Central (Rocamadour, Picodon, Pélardon), and from Provence (Banon, Tomme d'Annot, Brousse). One really is spoilt for choice!

Soft-curd cheeses with a bloomy rind (Camembert, Brie, Chaource) or washed rind (Maroilles, Livarot, Epoisses), rarely take less than a month to ripen. They are at their best on market stalls during the month of May.

Cheeses with pressed, uncooked curd (Saint-Nectaire, Reblochon) only come into peak condition later, since they need a longer ripening period. Sometimes they only reach their best in mid-June.

Hard-pressed cheeses (Comté, Beaufort Gruyère, Emmental), produced the previous summer, start to become very interesting. And the Tommes from the Auvergne or the Pyrenees do not lag far behind.

Among the delicious springtime specialities, Brousse du Rove is a strange little fresh cheese that is vigorously whisked before being moulded in long, narrow strainers, successors to the rams' horns probably used in the past.

CHEESES THROUGH THE SEASONS: THE BEST OF SUMMER

Cheeses are there for you in the summer. Don't hesitate to buy them. Most of those offered at this time of year were made in the middle or at the end of spring, when the milk was at its best. After maturing in the ripening cellars they arrive in tip-top condition on the retailer's shelves, which they enliven with their glowing quality. All the soft-curd cheeses are succulent. Their curd is unctuous, often creamy. The Camemberts are divine from July onwards, an appetizing golden-yellow colour inside. The Saint-Nectaires, after eight to ten weeks of ripening, are as plump and enticing as you could possibly wish, as are the Reblochons, who ask nothing better than to open their hearts to you. The Munsters, the Maroilles and the Pont l'Évêques are in glowing form. It is such a pity that people lose their appetite for cheese in the heat of the summer.

The goat's milk cheeses, accompanied by a rosé or a light red wine, are often the gourmets' choice. Select soft, tender ones. They will remain superb until the end of August as long as the grass doesn't become too parched by the summer sun. Cloudless summer skies quickly affect their quality.

All the fresh cheeses, whether made with cow's, goat's or ewe's milk, are pleasant to eat in hot weather. While they are enjoyable all the year round, they are particularly welcome in summer.

As for long-lasting cheeses, it is imperative to seek out those made the previous summer in mountain pastures. After maturing for a year their flavour is more and more pronounced and their full character begins to be revealed.

Summer is the ideal season in which to enjoy Munster.

CHEESES THROUGH THE SEASONS: THE BEST OF AUTUMN

For cheese, autumn is a second springtime, shorter but just as beneficial from the point of view of quality. The exhausted pastures, dried by the summer heat, are revived when rain returns and produce a second growth of grass. This rejuvenation coincides with the final few weeks of the animals' lactation period, a time when they normally produce richer milk. All this has an effect on the flavour and texture of the cheeses; thanks to the higher fat content they recover their supple texture. Some goat's milk cheeses, such as Sainte-Maure-de-Touraine, lose their lactic and grassy aromas and take on smoky flavours and those of dried fruit.

Cheeses produced by this 'second growth': from October onwards, cheeses made after

the grass has grown again in the pastures (which require only a short ripening period) begin to appear on the market stalls. The bloomy-rind ones are the first: Camemberts, Bries and so on. After that, allow yourself be carried away by the stronger aromas of washed-rind Reblochon, Saint-Nectaire, Livarot or Maroilles. But don't wait too long – by November they will begin to be past their best. As for goat's milk cheeses, many stockmen have now modified the breeding cycle so that the young are born in July and August, making the milk yield at its most abundant in September.

The spring cheeses. Also at their best are cheeses produced four or five months earlier, during the prosperous spring period, and now reaching maturity: blue cheeses such as Fourmes, Roquefort, Ossau-Iraty and so on.

Long-lasting cheeses. Made in the summer of the previous year, cheeses such as Comté, Beaufort and Gruyère are coming to full maturity. Time has improved them, developing the flavours deep within them.

The Mont-d'Ors are back, but the beginning of the season is not the best time for them. Wait until the first frosts before dipping your spoon into their little spruce boxes.

Cabrales (left) is the most famous of the Spanish blue-veined cheeses. It is unusual in that it is made principally from goat's milk.

CHEESES THROUGH THE SEASONS: THE BEST OF WINTER

Weather you wouldn't turn a cow or a goat out in… winter, when the pastures are denuded of grass and sodden with rain, is not the best time to make cheese. Many of the animals have gone dry and all are being fed on hay or, even worse, silage (fermented grass). For many cheeses it is a transitional period.

Without meaning to belittle them, those cheeses needing only short or medium ripening times (from two weeks to two months), which is to say the bulk of the soft ones, never quite manage to reach their peak. This is equally true of bloomy-rind cheeses (Camembert, Brie) and the washed rinds

(Pont l'Évêque, Livarot, Langres). As for goat's milk cheeses, there are none on the market stalls at this time.

Be on your guard during this period against cheeses made from frozen curd. They are inferior in quality and are easily recognizable by the fact that the rind tends to come away from the curd.

On the other hand, cheeses made in mountain regions in summer are presented in a very favourable light. You can throw in your lot with Ossau-Iraty, Salers, Laguiole or Appenzell without fear of disappointment. The long-lasting cheeses made the year before have had eighteen months in which to mature. They should really be at their best. Sumptuous Beauforts, Gruyères, Comtés are at their most inviting. The French name for winter, *hiver*, rhymes with Gruyère! And don't forget Mont d'Or, which is perfect from the end of December to mid-April.

Two cheeses which are delicious in winter: Beaufort and Morbier.
Left: Salting and rubbing the wheels of Beaufort in the cellars of the Guiguet cheese dairy in the Col des Saisies. This cheese can be recognized by its concave rind.
Opposite page: Making Morbier in the workshop of La Chapelle-du-Bois. The curd, once taken from the vat and collected into a ball, is just a shapeless mass.

CHOOSING CHEESES: KNOW HOW TO READ THE LABELS

Borrowed names: historically, some regions have either not known how, or been unable, to protect their local cheeses from imitation. The name escapes. This happened with Brie, Gruyère, Cheddar and Camembert, for example, which are now made all over the world. Once that has happened, the only remaining recourse is to protect a more geographically precise name, such as 'Sainte-Maure-de-Touraine' instead of 'Sainte-Maure', or 'Camembert de Normandie' instead of 'Camembert made in Normandie'. These are subtleties that could escape the notice of the consumer.

The invention of geographical names is as old as commerce itself. All that is needed is a name that sounds firmly rooted in a terroir – places which only exist, of course, on the label. Nobody is really fooled by them.

Freezing: while consumption of cheese is relatively constant, production is seasonal – a surfeit of milk being produced in spring. A current practice, totally unknown to consumers, is that of freezing the curd, especially for goat's milk cheeses and even some moulded cheeses, such as Saint-Nectaire. Both the taste and the texture of the cheeses can suffer from this practice but one will find no mention of freezing on the label. It is a form of lying by omission.

On the label, every word is important. Take the example of Camembert.

'Camembert de Normandie' indicates a genuine Camembert. It is covered by an AOC, obtained in 1983. It is strictly a product of raw Normandy milk, made in its terroir of origin and ladle moulded. Eleven cheese dairies make it.

'Camembert fabriqué en Normandie' may be made with raw or pasteurized milk and only the cheese dairy must be situated in Normandy – the milk may have originated elsewhere.

It may be that this product is of a perfectly acceptable quality, but it is far from offering all the intensity of that made with raw Normandy milk. It is reliable, but never exalted.

Finally, the simple 'Camembert', without any other indications, is a far cry from the real thing. The only thing in its favour is its very affordable price.

CHEESES MADE FROM RAW MILK: BEWARE OF COMMON MISCONCEPTIONS

The notion that cheeses made from raw milk carry a greater health risk than those made from pasteurized milk – especially that of contracting listeriosis – is firmly anchored in the minds of the consumer. However, this condemnation is totally unjustified; available epidemiological studies show that both are equally open to question. Listeria, a bacterium omnipresent in the environment, is harmless to the great majority of the population. It only presents a danger to certain, well-targeted 'at-risk' groups: pregnant women, who run the risk of spontaneous abortion, and people with weakened immune systems. For everyone else, listeria either has no effect or, at worst, causes passing tiredness and perhaps a slight fever. In addition, listeriosis only occurs if there is an abnormally high presence of the listeria bacterium. Pasteurization is no solution; a cheese in which the original microbiological content has been destroyed by this procedure is not immune to subsequent contamination. In this case, and unlike that of cheese made from raw milk in which there is a microbiological balance, the way is clear for the noxious bacteria to thrive. Real epidemics are rare. Listeriosis is a notifiable illness, which means that if several people are struck down by the same strain of listeria, the product that caused it can quickly be identified simply by asking the sufferers what they have eaten in the course of the previous weeks. Once traced, the product is withdrawn from sale. In the past, it needed a number of cases of listeriosis to trigger an alert. The most susceptible cheeses are the soft-curd ones with bloomy or washed rinds that are ripened only for a short period, (Camembert, Brie, Chaource, Époisses, Pont-l'Évêque, Livarot, Munster and so on). Products that are ripened for long periods, such as Roquefort, or the various Gruyères, pose no risk whatsoever.

San Marcellin cheeses draining.

CHEESES: HOW TO KEEP THEM IN PERFECT CONDITION

The two enemies of cheese are a dry atmosphere and changes in temperature. Here are a few rules to remember in order to avoid problems.

Keep them in the 'cellar' compartment of the refrigerator if it has one. The temperature is a few degrees higher than in the rest of the fridge and will maintain the cheese in good condition, away from cold draughts. Failing this, you should put them in the salad compartment, which retains the moisture.

Don't take cheeses out of the refrigerator too often; that way you will spare them constant changes in temperature and humidity, which tend to make them dry out.

Don't stock up for more than a week ahead. Few cheeses keep well for long periods, especially when they are at their peak. It is better to buy regularly from your cheese merchant, who is far better equipped to keep them in good condition. And buying more often, in smaller quantities, allows you to enjoy a greater variety.

Keep the cheeses wrapped, preferably in their original packaging. Most of them have a characteristic smell which can contaminate other products (butter, cream, liquids, certain fruits). Inversely, the fat in the cheese may well pick up the smells from other items stored with them. Also they risk cross-contamination: a Morbier could become covered with the white mould from a Camembert. Finally, an unwrapped cheese in a refrigerator (other than goat's milk cheeses) rapidly dries out. Cover the cut surfaces with cling film and the cheese will keep its flavour longer.

Avoid leaving cheese too long in sealed containers: the atmosphere is too confined.

A cloche serves more for presentation than preservation, other than for short periods, when it will slow down the temperature rise and thus the drying process. These items are often too large to put in the refrigerator, and also fail to separate the cheeses one from another.

Remember to get cheeses out an hour or two before they are needed – time to become acclimatized.

To conserve their unique flavour it is essential to store cheeses in the best possible conditions.

SENDING CHEESES: THE BEST METHOD

What should you do if friends ask you to send them a good Camembert made with raw milk? How can you send Comté and Saint-Nectaire – his favourite cheeses – to your son, who is on an exchange visit to New Caledonia?

Sealed in a package the cheeses risk suffering damage during the journey. The changes of temperature will inevitably accelerate the breakdown of the curd. Give preference, therefore, to hard-pressed cheeses, which develop more slowly than the soft-pressed ones. If you must send soft cheeses, send a whole cheese, so that it is protected by the rind, choose one that is not too ripe and keep it in its original wrapping. And leave it room to breathe. Put it in a polystyrene or cardboard box, allowing room for the air to circulate. A little powdered charcoal will help to stop some of the smell. And be careful, some countries regulate the importation of farm produce and your parcel could find itself held in customs.

Even without following the drastic regulations imposed on professionals (left: the dispatch room for *Manchego*, Spanish ewe's milk cheeses), cheeses can travel perfectly safely if you follow a few basic rules.

SERVING CHEESES: AN INTRODUCTION TO CUTTING THEM

The way cheeses are cut is governed by a combination of etiquette (respect both for the cheese and the other diners) and practical considerations both for using it and keeping it in good condition. A typical example of bad cheese manners is to cut yourself the piece from the centre of the Roquefort, where the 'blue' is most concentrated, and leaving the paler, blander outer part for the other diners. The rule requires that each helping of cheese should include a little of the rind – firstly so that everyone has a fair share, and secondly because the flavour of a cheese is never uniform throughout but usually more pronounced near the rind.

These nuances form part of the pleasure of eating it. There are a number of special tools for cutting cheese correctly. The *Roquefortaise*, made for cutting Roquefort, resembles a wire used for slicing butter and slices through the delicate cheese without crumbling it. As for the *girolle*, this allows one to cut shavings from a Swiss Tête-de-Moine. Some hard cheeses need a double-handed knife, while for soft cheeses a little curved, two-pronged knife is perfect. Don't hesitate to dip the knives into hot water before cutting blue cheeses, for instance. If you have none of these implements, then use a long knife with a rigid blade, augmented by a fork.

SERVING CHEESES: HOW MUCH PER PERSON?

The trick is to count the number of diners and divide by two, offering five cheeses for a table of ten people, for instance. But remember that it is imprudent to exceed ten cheeses on the board.

Making up a cheeseboard is a delicate operation. To please all the diners it is best to choose several kinds of cheese but this must be done carefully. Your cheese merchant will be able to advise you on good combinations. A single cheese chosen for its original character (like the Jonchées Niortaises below) is another possible solution, but be sure the flavour will appeal to all your guests.

SERVING CHEESES: A FEW WORDS ABOUT THE BOARD

The surface of the cheeseboard can be wood, wicker or marble, but never plastic or metal. It may be covered with straw before setting out the cheeses. The cheeses should be presented as simply as possible, without their boxes or wrappings (except in the case of Saint-Félicien, Vacherin and so on).

To make your cheeseboard look even more appetizing you could add cherry tomatoes, grapes, slices of apple, walnuts or raisins. Whatever takes your fancy.

Butter has its supporters and its detractors. Whatever your opinion, do let those who favour it succumb to the pleasure.

SAVOURING YOUR CHEESES: WHAT TO DO WITH THE RIND?

Chevrotins des Bauges, cheeses with a natural rind.

The rind is the protector of the cheese; it has its own texture and its own flavour, often much stronger than that of the rest of the cheese. (It is always salty.) A bloomy rind (Camembert, Brie and many goat's milk cheeses) generally gives off agreeable aromas of mushrooms. The washed rinds (regularly moistened in the ripening cellars) are the site of intense fermentation and delight lovers of strong smells and flavours. Brushed rinds (Tomme de Savoie) smell of the cellar and damp stone, and also have their followers. On the other hand, very thick rinds (Comté or Laguiole), or those coated in paraffin wax, are unfit to eat. One must refrain from giving too much advice in this matter – it is a question of personal preference. Some people maintain that the strong flavours of the rind can spoil one's perception of the subtler aromas of the cheese and should not be eaten for that reason. Others, on the contrary, think that it is an integral part of the character of the product. There is a risk that poor ripening may generate unpleasant tastes (ammonia, soap, bitterness and acrid flavours). The best way is simply to taste the rind and find out what it is like before deciding whether to eat it or not.

SAVOURING YOUR CHEESES: CHOOSING THE APPROPRIATE WINE

Wine, together with bread, is the best companion for cheese. But watch out for errors of taste and dubious combinations! Here are a few suggestions to surprise and enchant your taste buds.

Despite being common usage, serving red wine with cheese as a matter of course is a Pavlovian reflex which often does a disservice to both products. How many good bottles have been sacrificed to the cheese platter in this way, unable to express themselves and make themselves heard? It is true that the cheese comes at the end of the meal and we in France like to build up to a skilful climax, starting with the younger wines and working our way up to the oldest and most

prestigious – generally reds, but this can often lead to the finest wines being mishandled.

White wines, with their freshness and liveliness are, on the whole, better with cheese: Sauvignon with the goats' milk cheeses from Touraine and Berry; Gewurztraminer with Munster; Vin Jaune with Comté; Jurançon with Pyrenean ewe's milk cheeses; Marc de Bourgogne with Epoisse, etc. Equally, one could break away from the usual notions of marrying products from the same area and allow oneself to be seduced by some very unusual, but sumptuous combinations.

Did you know that Champagne is perfect with Parmesan and that Port enhances the quality of Beaufort? Or that the sweetness of Sauternes envelops and smoothes the rough edges of Roquefort, Banyuls gives nobility to a Bleu d'Auvergne and a delicate Vouvray adds structure to a Fourme d'Ambert? For a red wine chose a Burgundy rather than a Bordeaux. It's primarily a question of style; while Bordeaux wines are generally balanced and harmonious, Burgundies tend to be more straightforward, rougher, more voluptuous. Confronted with cheese, the finesse of a Bordeaux is often overshadowed by the lactic tones, whereas the bracing nature of Burgundy gives it greater control over the dominant acids. While Cabernet Sauvignon, frequently used in the making of Bordeaux, is one of the very tannic grape varieties, the Pinot Noir of Burgundy is much less so, giving more flowing, supple wines.

SAVOURING YOUR CHEESES: IN WHAT ORDER SHOULD YOU EAT THEM?

There you are, faced with a very tempting cheeseboard laden with five or six cheeses, perhaps even more. You have decided to do honour to all the great families with an unerring sense of geographic ecumenism: a goat's milk cheese from the Loire, a Gruyère from Savoie, a soft-pressed cheese with a washed rind from north-east France, blue-veined cheese from the Massif Central, a Pyrenean ewe's milk Tomme, a bloomy-rind cheese from Île de France. A few slivers of Mimolette and some rosettes of Tête-de-Moine from Switzerland to round it off. In which order should you savour this attractive array?

Keep your greedier instincts in check; they will lead you straight to your favourite cheese, unless you are the sort who keeps the best for the last. Consider instead the depth of flavour of each cheese – that is what will tell you the ideal order in which to taste them.

Begin with the cheeses with the most evanescent flavours (the fresh ones) and end with the strongest (a blue, a washed-rind or a well-matured pressed curd). The more mature – and therefore more intensely flavoured – they are, the more one must learn to keep them waiting.

A cheeseboard must be arranged with great care to offer freshness and originality and the promise of pleasure to come.

BREAD AND CHEESE: INSEPARABLE ALLIES

A leavened baguette or a country loaf; choose the type of bread according to the cheese it is to accompany.

If you serve only one kind of bread with the cheese, don't go in for anything too eccentric; it must please everybody, have a good flavour and go well with the cheeses offered. A good leavened baguette of the right quality would be perfect. Choose one with a crisp crust and a creamy crumb with plenty of holes. If you find baguette too commonplace, you could choose a good country loaf, made with yeast; that would go well with any kind of cheese.

Nut breads can be interesting. In some regions walnuts are automatically served with cheese, for their aroma is a perfect foil for the roasted or damp woodland notes found in some cheeses. Try some mature Comté with a Vin Jaune du Jura and nut-bread rolls. And you will find all these products playing in perfect harmony in exactly the same key.

Bread from a sandwich-type loaf is not suitable as it is too soft and relatively sweet, which detracts from the flavour of the cheese; at best it can be used spread with Crème de Roquefort to accompany an aperitif.

CHILDREN: INTRODUCING THEM TO CHEESE

Children's preferences for soft, insipid cheeses is often a reflection of their parents' prejudices, influenced by the 'gourmets in short trousers' school of advertising. But no biological factor exists that will automatically lead children to appreciate cheeses of character – they need to be shown the way. Children acquire their taste for different foods by imitating others; they copy their parents, their brothers and sisters and their friends, which shows how important are the role models held up to them. Sometimes they rebel and put on a sudden show of defiance (usually between two and three years of age),

even refusing food they ate happily before. This 'neophobia' reaches its peak when they are about five or six years old, and girls are more susceptible than boys. Just remember – never force children; give them time to get used to new ideas. Here are a few suggestions for helping to accustom children to the various flavours and textures of cheese.

Organize tasting games. You could put different cheeses on pieces of toast: blue cheese made with raw milk, Gruyère, Roquefort, etc. and invite them to smell and taste them, and question them about what they have eaten. They will tell you their impressions, in their own words, and will eventually finish by being able to tell the difference between ewe's milk and cow's milk cheeses – especially if you explain the nature of these animals.

Why not make them responsible for choosing the cheeses for a cheeseboard? Teach them about the different shapes and colours.

Put the cheeses that you teach them about in a geographical context, giving preference to those regions the child has already discovered.

Don't hesitate to take your children with you to the market, and get them to read the labels. That way they can learn to make their choice according to their tastes and preferences.

GOURMANDISM: WILL CHEESE REALLY PILE ON THE POUNDS?

Despite many improvements in the taste department, gourmets rarely enthuse about low-fat cheeses.

Cheese is often said to be a sinful indulgence for which we pay dearly in gained pounds. This impression is further reinforced by such stereotypes as the fat, jovial monks who so often adorn the labels. Cheese does, undeniably, contain fat; but not as much as is popularly believed, and in varying proportions according to the way it is made. The rule to remember is that the drier the cheese, the more concentrated the nutrients, the lipids in particular. In fact, a Camembert, with its very moist curd contains 22 per cent fat against 31 per cent in a Comté, with its much drier cooked pressed curd.

Since the fat in cheese is responsible for putting on weight, all that is needed is a low-fat product. This line of reasoning gave rise to cheeses 'lightened' by the use of milk skimmed to a greater or lesser degree. Unfortunately they have at least two drawbacks. First of all, their flavour puts them beyond the pale as far as gourmets are concerned. Fat is the element in cheese that carries the aroma and gives the curd its sensual texture; without it there is no pleasure in eating them. Secondly, our metabolism does not allow itself to be tricked for long. At each meal it carefully counts the calories consumed in order to regulate the appetite; if it is deceived by a low-fat item in the course of one meal, it will arrange to make up the difference at the next.

In my opinion, low-fat cheeses have half the fat and double the quantity of insipid matter for twice the price.

COOKING WITH CHEESE: MAKING RACLETTE

To stand up to the heat of the stove you need a relatively dry cheese that holds its shape and, above all, does not melt too quickly. Check the elasticity of the cheese – generally speaking that is the test of a cheese that will behave correctly under the influence of heat. The Valais cheeses are ideal but Appenzell, which is more readily available in France, is a good substitute. Certain of the Raclette cheeses from Franche-Comté or Savoie are not without merit, on condition that they are made from raw milk (absolutely essential) and are sufficiently matured. One could even try an Abondance. My colleague, Daniel Boujon, established at Thonon-les-Bains, recommends a raclette made with a very mature Vacherin Fribourgeois.

You need about 200 grams (7 ounces) of cheese per person. Add potatoes cooked in their skins (300 grams (10 ounces) per person), gherkins, small pickled onions and pepper. And why not include some *viande des Grisons* (a form of dried meat eaten in Switzerland) or raw ham?

To drink with your raclette: a Fendant du Valais, or a dry white wine from Savoie are heartily recommended. You could also drink tea with it, but never water, which hardens the cheese in the stomach and makes it difficult to digest.

See also Raclette Family, pages 122 to 129.

COOKING WITH CHEESE: MAKING FONDUE

When making fondue the Swiss often add cornflour or potato flour (once the cheese is completely melted). Not generally included in French recipes, both these ingredients produce a smooth and unctuous texture. They prevent the mixture from becoming elastic and sticky, especially if using less mature cheese. On the other hand, they can make it expand and turn frothy.

Mixing cheeses from different sources is an innovation thought up by imaginative, lowland cooks. For purists of the classical school, a real fondue needs only one type of cheese (and no cornflour!).

A successful mixture depends on the taste and texture you are aiming at. The first requirement is a good basic cheese with a fairly bland flavour (French Gruyère, Emmenthal). The other cheeses should contribute flavour and bind the mixture (Appenzell, Comté, Fribourg). Be sparing in the use of cheeses with a very high fat content – they give plenty of flavour but are difficult to digest.

For a perfect consistency the hard cheeses should be grated or cut into small cubes. The more supple cheeses can be cubed or cut into strips.

A fondue that is too liquid can be thickened by the addition of a little cornflour mixed with eau-de-vie or white wine. If too thick, add white wine to slacken it.

The wine to accompany it should be fairly dry, with a good acidity. It is considered smart to match cheeses and wines from the same area.

It is essential to serve bread that was made the previous day, or it will break down in the hot mixture and swell in the stomach.

The people of Franche-Comté habitually eat Mont d'Or in the form of a fondue. The recipe consists of immersing the cheese, still in its box, in cold water for fifteen minutes, to moisten the box and harden the cheese; a two-centimetre (one-inch) wide hollow is then made in the centre of the cheese and filled with white wine from the Jura before heating in a slow oven. The cheese becomes runny but the box, being damp, does not burn. The melted cheese is then poured over hot boiled potatoes and eaten with cold salamis, ham, etc.

COOKING WITH CHEESE: MAKING FONTAINEBLEAU AT HOME

It is possible to make Fontainebleau at home, on condition that you buy first-class ingredients: full-cream milk and full-fat crème-fraîche – preferably unpasteurized. One must bear in mind that Fontainebleau is an emulsion that is half way between a fresh white cheese and Chantilly cream.

Recipe for 4 servings:
First chill a bowl of the kind used for whisking egg whites, then put in 300 grammes (10 ounces) of crème fraîche and half a litre (18 fluid ounces) of milk – both full-fat and unpasteurized if possible. Mix together carefully with a hand whisk or failing that an electric mixer, and whisk in the same way as when beating egg whites for meringue. It will be immediately obvious if the cream or milk are unsuitable – the mixture will not emulsify. Semi-skimmed milk, for instance, will produce no reaction. Also, if the beating is done too rapidly there is a risk of the mixture turning to butter, so whisk it with wide, supple strokes until it emulsifies.

Left: Fontainebleau made in the traditional way at the Gorsat cheese dairy: the secret is in the way the *fromage frais* and the cream are whipped.
Note that a fresh cheese keeps only for a very short period; it should be eaten and enjoyed as soon as it is taken from the mould, after maturing for no more than 18 to 24 hours.

CAMEMBERT · BROCCIU · GOUDA · CHEDDAR · VENACO · CHAOURCE · VACHERIN · PÉLARDON · MANCHEGO · GRUYÈRE

1200
cheeses
100 favourites

The treasures of our cheese heritage

Classifications are not recognized in Nature. Grouping, sorting, cataloguing – these are bound to involve simplification and a certain deviation from the facts. The list of 1,200 cheeses that appears on the following pages is no exception.

It is constructed around fifty or so categories, each identified with one basic, representative cheese. Purists will no doubt feel that some of these groups are a trifle audacious and some more coherent than others. We have simply tried to look at this through the eyes of the vast number of consumers who ask us for 'a cheese of the such-and-such family'. Some of these 'families' are based on milk from one animal species, some on the shapes of the cheeses, others on a specific method of production. This attempt at simplification is aimed at making these annexes as readable and accessible as possible to all those lovers of good cheese who are put off by technical terms. The other difficulty we encountered – one common to any written material – is that of trying to work from a fixed point in a constantly changing landscape. Every day some products disappear and are replaced by others. Some, while retaining the same name, are produced by different methods. The scale on which some cheeses are produced can change, for example, from farmhouse cheeses made from raw milk to an industrial-style product using pasteurized milk. We hope the reader will forgive these errors or potential inaccuracies.

As far as possible we have given the precise geographical origin of each cheese, in the full knowledge that it may now be produced in a much wider area than that with which it is historically associated. For some cheeses more than one animal species is mentioned; these are made with a mixture of milks, on a regular or seasonal – or even alternating – basis. A number of cheeses are made in raw, pasteurized or partially-pasteurized milk versions. Some are covered by a Controlled Appellation of Origin (AOC) or its European equivalent, the Protected Appellation of Origin (AOP). This system of recognition, which began in France with Roquefort, is based on a product being very strongly rooted in a well-defined area. Little by little it has been taken up by other European countries (Switzerland only adopted it in the year 2000). Elsewhere, another European label, the IGP (protected geographic location), defines and protects those products which can claim a certain attachment to a specific *terroir*.

These appellations have not yet found favour in more distant regions, like North America or the Antipodes, where the idea of *terroir* is not given the same importance.

As for the optimum ripening periods indicated, these are based on personal opinion which should, of course, be qualified according to the product, the skill of the *affineur*, the season, etc. This list is not selected on the basis of quality or personal preference; many of the cheeses mentioned have never graced the shelves of Roland Barthélemy's establishment – nor ever will. Rather, its purpose is that of an inventory, to give an idea of the extraordinary diversity of our cheese heritage.

Cheese-producing countries

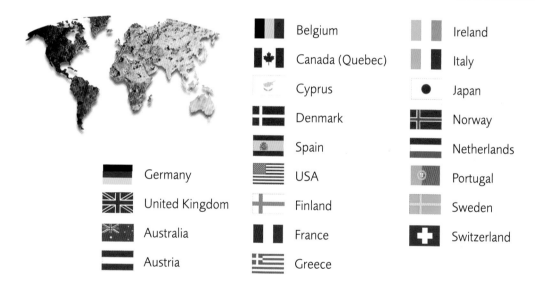

Belgium		Ireland
Canada (Quebec)		Italy
Cyprus		Japan
Denmark		Norway
Spain		Netherlands
Germany	USA	Portugal
United Kingdom	Finland	Sweden
Australia	France	Switzerland
Austria	Greece	

Milk-producing animals

Cow

Goat

Ewe

Buffalo

The Chaource family
and related cheeses

The cow's milk cheeses belonging to this family, made in the north-eastern region of France, characteristically have a fairly acidic, very fine-grained curd. They never become creamy as they mature.

Milk: R = raw, PP = partially pasteurized, P = pasteurized. Product: F = farmhouse, C = cottage industry, I = industrial.

Cheese	Other names	Country/Area of origin	Animal	Milk	Product	Label	Ripening
Bray picard		Picardy		R	C		1 month
Butte de Doué				P	C		1 month
Carré de Bray		Normandy		R, P	F, C, I		1 month
Chaource		Aube and Yonne		R, P	C	AOC-AOP	1 month
Maromme				R	F		1 month
Neufchâtel	Cœur de Bray	Bray region		R, P	F, C, I	AOC-AOP	3 weeks
Vignotte				P	C		1 month
Villebarou		Orleans region		R	F		2 months
Villedieu				R	F		1 month

The Époisses family
and related cheeses

This is the orange-coloured, washed rind version of the Chaource family, and has a much more pronounced flavour. Alcohol, or marc spirit is used in the ripening of some of these cheeses.

Milk: R = raw, PP = partially pasteurized, P = pasteurized. Product: F = farmhouse, C = cottage industry, I = industrial.

Cheese	Other names	Country/Area of origin	Animal	Milk	Product	Label	Ripening
Abbaye de la Pierre-qui-Vire		■ ■ Burgundy	🐄 🦌	R	C		1 month
Affidélis		■ ■ Burgundy	🐄	R, P	C		2 months
Aisy cendré	Cendré d'Aisy	■ ■ Burgundy	🐄	R	F, C		2 months
Ami du chambertin (L')		■ ■ Burgundy - Gevrey-Chambertin	🐄	R, P	C		2 months
Chablis		■ ■ Burgundy	🐄	P	C		2 months
Chaumont		■ ■ Champagne	🐄	R	C		3 months
Époisses		■ ■ Burgundy	🐄	R, PP, P	F, C	AOC-AOP	2 months
Langres		■ ■ Plateau de Langres	🐄	R, PP, P	F, C	AOC-AOP	2 months
Plaisir au chablis		■ ■ Brochon Côte-d'Or	🐄	P	C		1 month
Prestige de Bourgogne		■ ■ Burgundy	🐄	P	I		1 month
Soumaintrain		■ ■ Burgundy	🐄	R, P	F, C, I		2 months
Trou du cru	Cœur d'époisses	■ ■ Burgundy	🐄	R, T	C		1 month

Langres
France (Champagne-Ardenne)
Cow's milk

Small in stature but with a big character! Langres is a cheese from the Champagne region; its Appellation zone is centred on the Langres plateau, a big grazing area. It has a curious hollow in the centre of its rind – the 'fountain' – that deepens as the whey drains from the cheese, which is never turned over during ripening. This feature is the best indicator of ripeness in a Langres; the deeper the hollow the riper the cheese. It is at its best when the hollow is five millimetres (0.2 inch) deep, by which time the curd is dense and has a melting quality, and the flavour is expansive without being strong. It is regularly rubbed with salt solution, every two days or so, to help foster the growth of the 'red ferment' that gives it its orange colour and encourages the flavour to develop. Langres goes back a long way; it almost disappeared in the 1950s but now four producers are working towards its re-establishment, including enterprising farmer Claudine Gillet, at Modia Farm who, with the help of her family, keeps about a hundred dairy cows. She tells me that in the past Langres was simply a fresh white cheese, drained in earthenware moulds and ripened no more than a few days, when it became dry and yellowed. Nowadays consumers prefer it ripe and very creamy. Before eating it, I suggest you pour a few drops of Champagne, or marc de Bourgogne into its hollow.

Family
Époisses
Country
France
Area of origin
The Langres Plateau
Animal species
Cow
Milk
Raw, partially pasteurized, pasteurized
Product
Farmhouse or cottage industry
Optimum ripening
2 months

Pierre-qui-Vire

France (Burgundy)
Cow's or goat's milk

In the north of the regional park at Morvan, between Avallon and Saulieu, Pierre-qui-Vire Abbey has given over the production of its cheese and the care of its herds of sixty Alpine Brown cows and sixty goats of the Alpine breed to lay workers. The abbey has returned to this traditional function after a bruising set-back in the 1960s, when it acquired high-yielding dairy cattle (Friesians) and intensified production. In 1969 it converted to environmentally friendly, sustainable agriculture. The animals are essentially fed on fresh grass and hay, the use of silage having been given up three years ago. Pierre-qui-Vire cheese was created in the post-war years on a farm the monks had set up to produce milk for the pupils of their boarding school. This cheese is made either with cow's milk (produced all year round), or goat's milk (from 15th February to 15th December). Its recipe is similar to that of Époisses, though it is ripened differently. The cheese is more or less the size of a Camembert, its bloomy orange rind is coloured with *rocou*, a natural colouring from Mexico, and its texture is quite creamy. It is eaten fairly fresh (ripened for one to two weeks maximum), but there is also a Pierre-qui-Vire 'au Chablis', which is ripened for longer. This I recommend.

Family
Époisses
Country
France
Area of origin
Burgundy
Animal species
Cow, goat
Milk
Raw
Product
Cottage industry
Optimum ripening
1 month

Soumaintrain

France (Burgundy)
Cow's milk

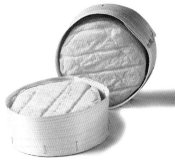

Family
Époisses
Country
France
Area of origin
Burgundy
Animal species
Cow
Milk
Raw or pasteurized
Product
Farmhouse, cottage
industry or industrial
Optimum ripening
2 months •

Soumaintrain is an ancient cheese that was re-launched about fifteen years ago after almost disappearing. The farm production, quite considerable in the last century, practically closed down. The project was finally given a boost by the milk quotas that incited three young farmers to make a more profitable use of their milk (it needs three litres (five pints) to make one Soumaintrain). I followed with great interest the efforts of Claude Leroux, *affineur* at Brion, who actively encouraged the resurrection of this rustic-looking cheese, largely sold locally, and now collects the produce of five farms. This very characteristic cheese is made in a similar way to Époisses – the same fairly fine-grained curd, the same ochre, sometimes sticky rind, frequent washing (two or three times a week) to encourage the appearance of 'red ferment', clear evidence of quality. The basic difference is that Soumaintrain is not macerated in alcohol. Claude Leroux keeps it for a minimum of eighteen days – there are those who prefer it young – and up to two months for lovers of strong flavours. It can need boxing when it is very mature (some people melt it in the oven before eating it with potatoes). The Soumaintrain that is made in springtime is really excellent. Claude advises eating it as an early snack in the morning, with a glass of Chablis.

Many of the cheeses that form part of our European cheese heritage, including Pierre-qui-Vire (page 39) or this Munster (opposite page), were originally created by monks.

The Brie de Meaux family
and related cheeses

This family of cheeses originated to the east of Paris.
It consists of elegant discs of cow's milk cheese covered
in a fine white down (bloomy rind). The texture of these
cheeses delights in turning creamy as it matures.

Milk: R = raw, PP = partially pasteurized, P = pasteurized. Product: F = farmhouse, C = cottage industry, I = industrial.

Cheese	Other names	Country/Area of origin	Animal	Milk	Product	Label	Ripening
Bath cheese	Bath soft cheese	Avon	cow	R, P	C		1 month
Melbury			cow	P	I		2 months
Sharpam		Devon	cow	R	F		2 months
Somerset brie		Somerset	cow	P	I		1 month
Grape vine aash brie		New South Wales	cow	P	C		1 month
Jindi brie		Victoria	cow	P	F		1 month
Timboon farmhouse blue		Victoria	cow	P	C		2 months
Vermont farmhouse brie		Vermont	cow	P	I		1 month
Brie			cow	P	I		1 month
Brie de Coulommiers	Brie petit moule	Seine-et-Marne	cow	R	C, I		2 months
Brie de Macquelines		Île-de-France	cow	P	C		2 months
Brie de Malesherbes		Seine-et-Marne	cow	R	C		6 weeks
Brie de Meaux	Brie de Valois	Seine-et-Marne	cow	R	C, I	AOC-AOP	3 months
Brie de Melun		Seine-et-Marne – Brie	cow	R	F, C, I	AOC-AOP	3 months
Brie de Montereau		Île-de-France	cow	R	C		2 months
Brie de Nangis		Île-de-France	cow	R	C		2 months
Brie de Provins		Île-de-France	cow	R	C		2 months
Brie fermier		Île-de-France	cow	R	F		2 months
Brie noir		Île-de-France	cow	R	C		6 months
Chevru		Île de France	cow	R, P	C		3 months
Fougeru		Île-de-France	cow	R	C, I		1 month
Abbey blue brie			cow	R	F		2 months
Dunbarra			cow	P	I		1 month
Pencarreg		Cardiganshire	cow	P	C		1 month

Brie de Malesherbes
France (Île-de-France)
Cow's milk

In 1982, when I acquired the former town milk depot at Fontainebleau, I found old documents and heard local old people's accounts of a technique for ripening 'Brie des Moissons' – a cheese I undertook to resuscitate. Its origins – on the sandy plain of Montereau, in the Seine-et-Marne region – go back to the nineteenth century. This is a poorer area for cattle farming than the rich dairy zones of Brie further to the north, and since there was less milk, the farmers made their cheeses smaller – 800 grams (28 ounces) (against about 2.6 kilos (5 pounds 10 ounces)) for a Brie de Meaux, for example. There was one notable cheesemaker at a place called Ville-Saint-Jacques, near Montereau. This little cheese, which the men took with them when they went fishing, or to work in the fields, was rolled in ash to preserve it and had a very pronounced flavour. The one we recreated, using organic charcoal, is more to modern taste. I couldn't call it Brie de Ville-Saint-Jacques as that name was already in use for a commercial product, so I opted for Brie de Malesherbes, the name of the milk depot in Fontainebleau, which was subsequently taken over by Gilles and Odile Goursat, nephew and niece of my wife Nicole. The Brie de Malesherbes is in good hands.

Family
Brie de Meaux
Country
France
Area of origin
Seine-et-Marne
Animal species
Cow
Milk
Raw
Product
Cottage industry
Optimum ripening
6 weeks

Brie de Melun
France (Île de France)
Cow's milk

Family
Brie de Meaux
Country
France
Area of origin
Seine-et-Marne, Brie
Animal species
Cow
Milk
Raw
Product
Farmhouse, cottage
industry or industrial
Optimum ripening
3 months

With red streaks peeking through the white bloom on its rind, Brie de Melun is the most rustic of the French Bries. One of the oldest, too, since it originated at least a thousand years ago. It is stronger flavoured, saltier and more characteristic than the rather more refined Brie de Meaux. While the latter enjoys long-standing success and is known all over the world, Brie de Melun has never had a conquering instinct, nor any inclination to travel. For a long time it was a farmhouse cheese, made for domestic consumption, as its size – smaller than Brie de Meaux – indicates. A longer coagulation time and a ripening technique that brings out the 'red ferment' explains its character. It has always been very tricky to handle, its saltiness being quick to gain the upper hand. Traditionally it was sold fairly young, barely ripened. I like to ripen it for eight to ten weeks. One can also find some that have been ripened for even longer, but they become dry, darker and with very strong flavour, reminiscent of the 'harvest Bries' – inferior cheeses that were left to dry and given to the workers in the fields. The *Confrérie du Brie de Melun* (brotherhood of Brie de Melun) never fails to celebrate this tradition at the end of spring.

Fougeru
France (Île de France)
Cow's milk

This cheese was invented in the 1960s by Robert
Rouzaire, cheesemaker and *affineur* in the
Seine-et-Marne region. It is rather like a large
Coulommier decorated with fern leaves.
The leaves are collected between April and
May, some distance away in the Loir-et-Cher
forests near the town of Amboise; the ferns that
grow in Île-de-France are not suitable because they
fade too quickly. This creamy cheese is made from
raw milk and hand-moulded by ladle. The milk, partially
skimmed, is used as fresh as possible. It needs six to
seven litres (10.5 to 12 pints) of milk to make one
Fougeru. Because it is a relatively thick cheese
(3.5 centimetres (1.3 inches) and 16 centimetres (6 inches)
in diameter), drainage of the whey does not happen
automatically, so Fougeru is subject to a very special
ripening technique, the secret of which is jealously guarded
by the Rouzaire Company. The cheese must be ripened for
at least two weeks. Very much enjoyed for its supple texture,
Fougeru can be eaten while the centre is still slightly chalky.
It is a cheese that will do credit to any cheeseboard and is
especially sought-after for the festive table at Christmas,
New Year and Easter.

Family
Brie de Meaux
Country
France
Area of origin
Île-de-France
Animal species
Cow
Milk
Raw
Product
Cottage industry or industrial
Optimum ripening
1 month

The Camembert family
and related cheeses

A descendant of Brie, it is smaller and thicker. Its convenient format was an important factor in the rapid development of its popularity. A great many versions of it are made worldwide.

Milk: R = raw, PP = partially pasteurized, P = pasteurized. Product: F = farmhouse, C = cottage industry, I = industrial.

Cheese	Other names	Country/Area of origin	Animal	Milk	Product	Label	Ripening
Weisse lady		Bavaria		P	I		1 month
Somerset Camembert		Somerset (England)		P	C		1 month
Waterloo		Berkshire (England)		R	C		1 month
Bouquet des moines				P	C		1 month
Bonchester		Roxburghshire (Scotland)		R, PP	C	AOC-AOP	2 months
Teviotdale		Scotland		R, PP	C	AOC-AOP	3 months
Airiños		Asturias		P	C		1 month
Barberey	Fromage de Troyes	Champagne		R, P	C		1 month
Belle-des-champs				P	I		3 weeks
Bouysette		Rouergue		R	F		3 weeks
Brillador				P	I		1 month
Brique de Jussac				P	C		1 month
Briquette de Coubon		Auvergne		R	F		3 weeks
Camembert		Southern Normandy		P	I		3 weeks
Camembert au calvados		Normandy		R	C		1 month
Camembert de Normandie		Normandy		R	F, C, I	AOC-AOP	1 month
Caprice des dieux		Champagne		P	I		2 weeks
Carré				P	I		1 month
Carré de l'est		Lorraine-Champagne		P	I		1 month
Carré de Lorraine		Lorraine		P	I		1 month
Cendré d'Argonne		Champagne-Ardenne		P	C		2 months
Cendré de Champagne	Fromage cendré	Champagne-Ardenne		R, P	C		1 month
Chécy		Orleans region		P	C		1 month
Chiberta		Basque country		P	C		1 month
Colombier		Burgundy-Auxois		R	F		1 month
Coulommiers		Île-de-France		R, P	C, I		1 month
Crème des prés				P	I		1 month

Cheese	Other names	Country/Area of origin	Animal	Milk	Product	Label	Ripening
Crémet du cap Blanc-Nez	Cap blanc-nez	Nord-Pas-de-Calais		R	F		3 weeks
Évry-le-châtel		Champagne		R, P	C		1 month
Feuille de Dreux	Dreux à la feuille Marsauceux	Dreux		R, P	C		1 month
Feuille de sauge		Orleans region		P	C		1 month
Frinault		Orleans region		P	C		1 month
Galette des monts du Lyonnais		Lyons region		R	C		3 weeks
Géramont				P	I		1 month
Henri IV				P	I		1 month
Olivet bleu		Loiret		R, PP, P	C		1 month
Olivet cendré		Loiret		R, PP, P	C		1 month
Olivet foin		Loiret		R, PP, P	C		1 month
Oreiller de ciboulette				P	C		1 month
Pannes cendré		Loiret		R, P	C		3 months
Pas de l'escalette		Southern Aveyron		R	F		1 month
Patay		Loiret		P	C		2 months
Pavé d'affinois				P	I		1 month
Petit-bessay		Bourbonnais		R	F		1 month
Petit camembert au calva		Normandy		R	F, C, I		1 month
Pithiviers au foin	Bondaroy au foin	Loiret		P	I		1 month
Riceys	Cendré des Riceys	Champagne		R	C		2 months
Rigotte de sainte-colombe		Savoy		P	C		3 weeks
Saint-benoît		Orleans region		R	C		1 month
Saint-félicien		Vivarais		R, P	F, C, I		1 month
Saint-marcellin		Dauphiné		R, PP, P	F, C, I		1 month
Saint-morgon		Mayenne		P	I		15 days
Tomme de Romans	Romans	Drôme and Ardèche		P	C, I		15 days
Val des moines				P	I		1 month
Vendôme cendré	Vendôme bleu	Orleans region		R	F		12 months
Voves				P	C		2 months
Cooleeney		Tipperary		R	F		6 weeks
Saint Killian		Wexford		R	C		1 month
Formaggella		Italian Sub-Alps		P	I		1 month
Tomme de Rougement		Vaud canton		R	C		3 weeks
Tomme vaudoise				R, PP, P	C		3 weeks

Cendré de Champagne
France (Champagne-Ardenne)
Cow's milk

These 'cendré' cheeses are part of a great tradition of the Champagne region linked to work in the vineyards. They were intended for the vineyard workers, particularly at harvest time. For the local cheesemakers, ash was the best medium for keeping their produce over a period of months. The cheeses were rolled and stored in chests filled with the ash from burnt vine prunings and other kinds of wood. From Troyes to the Ardennes, one finds numerous variants of this (something similar is produced in the Orleans area). These Cendrés have gradually died out with the advent of refrigeration. The basic recipe in those areas bordering the Aube and Chaource resembled that of Coulommiers; in those nearer to Burgundy, that of Époisses.

Their flavour, it seems, was quite pronounced. One of those which has stood the test of time is Cendré d'Aisy, a cheese of the Époisses type made to the north of Dijon. The ash is only applied to the cheeses now after they are fully ripened, just to give them the 'cendré' appearance.

Family
Camembert
Other name
Fromage Cendré
Country
France
Area of origin
Champagne-Ardenne
Animal species
Cow
Milk
Raw or pasteurized
Product
Cottage industry
Optimum ripening
1 month

Coulommiers
France (Île-de-France)
Cow's milk

This cheese is something between a Camembert and a Brie. Coulommiers certainly originated in the Brie area, to the east of Paris, home of the present-day Brie de Meaux and Brie de Melun. Like them, its texture is perfectly unctuous, but its size – only about 13 centimetres (5 inches) in diameter – and its greater thickness give it the appearance of a large, flattened Camembert. This format, easier to transport to Paris markets than the larger, fragile and difficult-to-handle Brie, was responsible for its rapid development and great success in the nineteenth century. Coulommiers has copied Camembert's chunky format, but does not quite match its Norman relative's fulsome flavour. This is hardly surprising since, for the most part, it is now produced from pasteurized milk. Not covered by an AOC, it can be made anywhere in France, though in fact it is mostly made by the producers of Brie de Meaux or Brie de Melun, established in a wide area running from the Seine-et-Marne region to the Meuse. Ideally Coulommiers should be ripened for up to two months. The reddish streaks that may appear on the white rind during this time are a reliable indication of a more pronounced flavour and a very creamy texture. Watch out for them.

Family
Camembert
Country
France
Area of origin
Île-de-France
Animal species
Cow
Milk
Raw or pasteurized
Product
Cottage industry or industrial
Optimum ripening
1 month

Feuille de Dreux

France (Centre)
Cow's milk

Right up to the end of the Second World War, Feuille de Dreux, also called Dreux à la Feuille, did duty as a midday snack for the agricultural workers employed by cereal-producers at Beauce. It was a domestic cheese, disc-shaped and made from skimmed milk, often with a greyish rind and a sometimes very strong flavour. An unpretentious, rustic cheese, it was surmounted by a leaf. Today only one cheesemaker makes Feuille de Dreux and the cheese has gone up-market; it now resembles a larger but thinner Coulommier with a white rind. In Chartres, it is known simple as Le Dreux or Le Marsauceux – the name of a little town in Eure-et-Loire that used to produce a famous cheese. The chestnut leaf laid on the rind, now purely for decoration, was traditionally used to separate the cheeses and prevent them sticking to each other during ripening. In the country the locals use Dreux for a very unusual concoction called *fromagée*. This consists of strips of cheese layered with pepper, moistened with cider or alcohol and macerated for two weeks, hermetically sealed in an earthenware dish. A way of resuscitating cheeses that are past their best that results in a pretty strong flavour!

Family
Camembert
Other names
Dreux à la Feuille,
Marsauceux
Country
France
Area of origin
Dreux
Animal species
Cow
Milk
Raw or pasteurized
Product
Cottage industry
Optimum ripening
1 month

Olivet Cendré

France (Centre)
Cow's milk

Olivet is the name of a small town on the river Loiret, near Orleans. It has produced a cheese that was very popular in the countryside, especially the wine-producing areas. About the size of a Camembert, this cheese served mainly as the staple food of the seasonal workers at the time of the grape-harvest. To supply this need, the cheesemakers preserved the cheeses made in the spring, when there was an abundance of milk, by rolling them in the ash from burnt vine clippings. This deterred insects and rodents of all kinds and stopped mould from forming on the rinds and ripening the cheeses too quickly. Moulds tend to develop very easily on this type of cheese – originally made with lactic curd, but nowadays with rennet. There is also an 'Olivet Bleu' which is not *cendré*. While the processes are no longer the same, the recipe for Olivet has been passed down intact, the ash now being replaced by the much darker powdered charcoal. Strictly speaking, I suppose one ought to call it Olivet 'Charbonné' ('charcoaled'). There is also an Olivet au Foin (hay), strewn with a few wisps of straw. This cheese, made with partially skimmed milk, needs a proper ripening period of about a month to bring out its flavour; cow's milk cheeses always need a little time to develop their full potential.

Family
Camembert
Country
France
Area of origin
Loiret
Animal species
Cow
Milk
Raw, partially pasteurized or pasteurized
Product
Cottage industry
Optimum ripening
1 month

Petit Camembert au Calva

France (Southern Normandy)
Cow's milk

It was my Auvergne compatriot, Henry Vergnes, from the Au Sauvignon bistro in Paris, who gave me the idea of this miniature Camembert macerated in Calvados. These two great products of the Normandy *terroir* have long been linked. There are also excellent Camemberts macerated in cider. I asked Philippe Meslon, from the Saint-Loup-de-Fribois cheese dairy, near Cambremer, to make a special batch of Camemberts from raw milk, 5 centimetres (2 inches) in diameter and 2 centimetres (0.7 inches) high. He had to have the moulds specially made. Because of their small size, these cheeses ripen more quickly than traditional Camemberts. After three weeks they are ready and are left to macerate for 24 hours in Calvados. Thus impregnated, they are then rolled in fine breadcrumbs (no need to remove the rind), then each one is tied with a little green ribbon and decorated with half a shelled walnut. Result: 60 grams (2 ounces) of pure pleasure which is gone in two mouthfuls. Its size makes it the 'petit four' of the cheese world. Perfect as a midday snack, it also makes an attractive addition to the cheeseboard.

Family
Camembert
Country
France
Area of origin
Normandy
Animal species
Cow
Milk
Raw
Product
Farmhouse, cottage industry or industrial
Optimum ripening
1 month

Saint-Félicien

France (Rhône-Alpes)
Cow's milk

This is an enriched version of Saint-Marcellin, in a slightly larger format. Two cheese merchants are both credited with having created it, one at Lyons and the other at Villeurbanne. This absolutely delightful cheese comes in a raw version, a pasteurized version, and a third one made from raw milk and pasteurized cream. In the absence of a blueprint giving a precise definition of this cheese, everyone makes it in their own way. Its delicious smell of cream, its creamy texture, its slightly ridged rind, tinged with blue mould, really make the mouth water. It is particularly full-flavoured in spring, when its fresh cream smell is very pronounced. Great care must be taken when ripening this type of product; it can quickly get out of hand and develop defects, of which the most usual is a soapy taste under the rind. Because of the success of their product, and in the face of competition from industrial copies, the eleven makers of this cheese, almost all of whom also produce Saint-Marcellin, are beginning to look for some sort of official recognition. Be warned: there is also a Saint-Félicien made in the Ardèche from goat's milk and not enriched.

Family
Camembert and Pélardon
Country
France
Area of origin
Vivarais
Animal species
Cow
Milk
Raw or pasteurized
Product
Farmhouse, cottage industry or industrial
Optimum ripening
1 month

Saint-Marcellin

France (Rhône-Alpes)
Cow's milk

Family
Camembert
Country
France
Area of origin
Dauphiné
Animal species
Cow
Milk
Raw, partially pasteurized
or pasteurized
Product
Farmhouse, cottage
industry or industrial
Optimum ripening
1 month

Dating back several centuries, it used to be made with goat's milk, but Saint-Marcellin is now exclusively cow's milk. Nanny goats browsing cheaply on roadside grass verges have progressively disappeared from the countryside. This cheese, deliciously creamy when well ripened, has always attracted prestigious patrons. The governor of the Dauphiné – the future Louis XI – assured its future in 1445 when, after a spirited hunt, he found himself alone and facing a bear. He was rescued by two woodcutters, who later introduced him to the local cheese, which delighted him. Demand took off when the railway arrived at Saint-Marcellin between 1860 and 1870, giving access to big city markets. The supply of goat's milk, by then no longer sufficient, was augmented with cow's milk; after a few decades it was abandoned completely.

At Lyons, Paul Bocuse and La Mère Richard did a great deal to popularize Saint-Marcellin, which was soon granted an AOC centred on the Dauphiné. This cheese is at its best and quite irresistible when made with the rich spring milk. It needs to be served in a small, deep dish. I choose those from the Etoile de Vercors cheese dairy, where some of the *hâloirs* (ripening rooms) give directly onto the Isère – the river that runs beside the dairy. The atmosphere is perfect for these cheeses, which like humidity.

Making Camembert: it needs four to five ladlefuls to fill each mould.

The Munster Family
and related cheeses

All these cheeses have very strong characteristics caused by the washing of the rind during ripening, which encourages the development of 'red ferment'. They readily become soft and runny.

Milk: R = raw, PP = partially pasteurized, P = pasteurized. Product: F = farmhouse, C = cottage industry, I = industrial.

Cheese	Other names	Country/Area of origin	Animal	Milk	Product	Label	Ripening
Andescher		Bavaria		P	C		3 months
Knappenkäse				P	I		2 months
Münster		Black Forest		R, P	C, I		2 months
Romadur	Romadurkäse			P	I		2 months
Weinkäse				P	I		2 months
Weisslaacker Bierkäse	Weisslacker			P	I		2 months
Stinking Bishop		Gloucestershire		P	C		2 months
Polkolbin smear ripened				P	C		6 weeks
Bierkäse				P	C		3 months
Mondseer		Salzburg region		P	C		2 months
Schlosskäse				P	I		2 months
Beaux prés				P	I		2 months
Fromage de Bruxelles	Brusselse kaas	Brabant		P	I		1 month
Herve	Herve kaas	Herve		R, P	C, I	AOC-AOP	3 months
Remedou	Piquant	Liège region		P	F, C		4 months
Ange cornu		Quebec region		R	F		2 months
Laracam		Lanaudière		R	C		3 months
Lechevalier-Mailloux		Quebec region		R	F		2 months
Pied-de-vent		Îles-de-la-Madeleine		R	F		2 months
Pont couvert		Mauricie-Bois-Francs		R	C		2 months
Bishop Kennedy		Perthshire		R	C, I		2 months
Tetilla		Galicia		P	C, I	AOC-AOP	2 months
Tronchón		La Mancha		P	F, C		2 months
Ulloa		Galicia		P	I		1 month
Liederkranz				P	I		2 months
Baguette laonnaise	Baguette de Thiérache	Picardy		P	I		3 months
Bergues		Flanders coast		R	F, C		2 months

Cheese	Other names	Country/Area of origin	Animal	Milk	Product	Label	Ripening
Chaumes		Dordogne-Pyrenees	cow	P	I		1 month
Cœur d'Arras		Artois	cow	P	C		1 month
Cœur d'Avesnes		Nord	cow	P	C		1 month
Cœur de Thiérache		Picardy	cow	P	C		1 month
Craquegnon affiné à la bière 'la gauloise'		Nord	cow	R	C		3 months
Crayeux de Roncq		Flanders	cow	R	F		2 months
Creux de Beaufou		Vendée	cow	R	F		2 months
Croquin de la Mayenne		Mayenne	cow	P	C		3 weeks
Curé nantais	Fromage du pays nantais – Petit breton – Fromage du curé	Nantes region	cow	P	C, I		1 month
Dauphin		Flanders	cow	R, P	C, I		4 months
Fleur de bière		Meurthe-et-Moselle	cow	P	C		1 month
Fromage de foin		Picardy	cow	R	F		3 months
Fromage fort de Béthune		Flanders	cow	R	C		3 months
Gauville		Normandy	cow	R, PP, P	F		2 months
Gérardmer		Vosges	cow	P	I		2 months
Gris-de-Lille	Puant macéré – Vieux-lille – Maroilles gris – Vieux-gris-de-Lille	Flanders	cow	R, P	C, I		4 months
Guerbigny		Picardy	cow	R	C		1 month
Le quart (maroilles)		Nord	cow	R, PP, P	F, C	AOC-AOP	3 months
Lisieux	Petit lisieux	Pays d'Auge	cow	R, PP, P	C, I		2 months
Livarot	Colonel	Pays d'Auge	cow	R, PP, P	C, I	AOC-AOP	2 months
Losange-de-saint-pol		Nord	cow	R	C		3 months
Mamirolle		Doubs	cow	P	C		15 days
Maroilles		Nord et Aisne	cow	R, P	F, C	AOC-AOP	4 months
Mignon (maroilles)		Flanders	cow	R	F	AOC-AOP	3 months
Mignot	Mignot blanc	Pays d'Auge	cow	R	F		2 months
Munster	Géromé	Vosges	cow	R, PP, P	F, C, I	AOC-AOP	3 months
Pas de l'Ayau		Nord	cow	R	C		2 months
Pavé d'Auge	Pavé de Moyaux	Southern Normandy	cow	R, P	F, C		3 months
Pavé de Moyeux		Normandy – Pays d'Auge	cow	R, P	F, C		2 months
Pavé du Plessis		Northern Normandy	cow	R	C		3 months
Pont-l'évêque		Normandy	cow	R, PP, P	F, C, I	AOC-AOP	2 months
Récollet		Lorraine	cow	P	C		1 month

Cheese	Other names	Country/Area of origin	Animal	Milk	Product	Label	Ripening
Rigotte d'Échalas		Lyons region		P	C		3 weeks
Rigotte de Condrieu		Lyons region		R	F		1 month
Rigotte des Alpes		Dauphiné, Lyons region		P	I		2 weeks
Rigottes		Dauphiné, Lyons region, Loire		R, P	C		1 month
Rocroi	Cendré des Ardennes	Ardennes		R	F		2 months
Rollot	Cœur de rollot	Picardy		R, P	F, C, I		2 months
Roucoulons		Franche-Comté		P	I		1 month
Rougette				P	I		1 month
Rouy		Burgundy		P	I		1 month
Saint-albray		South-West		P	I		3 weeks
Saint-aubin		Anjou		P	I		1 month
Saint-rémy		Franche-Comté – Vosges		P	I		2 months
Saulxurois		Champagne-Ardenne		PP	C		2 months
Sorbais (maroilles)		Flanders		R	F	AOC-AOP	3 months
Tomme de Séranon		Provence		R	F		3 weeks
Trouville		Normandy		P	C		2 months
Vacherol				P	I		3 months
Vieux-boulogne		Boulogne region		R	C		2 months
Vieux pané		Mayenne		P	I		3 weeks
Vieux-boulogne		Boulogne region		R	C		3 months
Void		Lorraine		P	C		3 months
Ardrahan		Cork		P	C		2 months
Brescianella		Lombardy		P	C		3 months
Quartirolo lombardo		Lombardy		R, P	F, C	AOC-AOP	1 month
Robiola della Valsasina		Lombardy		P	C		3 weeks
Salva		Lombardy		R, P	C		3 months
Taleggio		Piedmont, Lombardy, Veneto		R, P	C, I	AOC-AOP	2 months

Bergues

Northern France

Cow's milk and whey

Bergues is a spruce little walled town, inland from Dunkirk, whose abbey survived – more or less well – fire and pillage. There is no doubt that Bergues cheese, made to a recipe taken from the Trappiste cheeses, was created within the abbey walls at the end of the Middle Ages. Characteristically it is made from skimmed milk and whey and is washed frequently in salt water and beer, which gives it a strong odour that surprises some cheese lovers and could even put them off. That would be a mistake. On the palate, Bergues is very much milder than the smell would suggest. It had difficulty in establishing its identity and for a long time was thought to be an imitation of a Dutch cheese – but only an approximate one, because its makers couldn't get the curd to harden sufficiently. Produced in very limited numbers about thirty years ago, it now seems to have been rescued; it is made by eight farmers and its recipe has become well established. A good ripening period is thirty days and it is done in semi-basement cellars (it is difficult to dig deep foundations in that part of Flanders) called 'hoffsteads'. I suggest you go to Bergues market on a Monday to discover the honest, characteristic flavour of this cheese that is the delight of sailors in Northern France.

Family
Munster
Country
France
Area of origin
Coastal Flanders
(Dunkirk region)
Animal species
Cow
Milk
Raw
Product
Farmhouse or
cottage industry
Optimum ripening
2 months

Coeur d'Arras

Northern France
Cow's milk

Philippe Olivier, my fellow *affineur* from Boulogne-sur-Mer, told me the following anecdote. When the town of Arras was under Spanish rule, the occupying forces put notices up on the town gates saying: 'When the French take Arras, the mice will eat the cats'. The town was finally taken by Turenne in 1654, after a century and a half of occupation. The people of Arras posted the response: 'When the French give up Arras, the mice will eat the cats'. Every year at Whitsuntide, the Feast of the Rats is held to commemorate these historic events. The name of the fête probably comes from a bad pun (*à rats* is pronounced the same as Arras in French), but it could equally refer to the claim that the Spaniards let rats loose in the town. But be that as it may, on this occasion the local specialities are on show and, traditionally, they are all – chocolate, gingerbread, etc. – made in the form of a heart. It was inevitable that a cheese should also be produced in that shape, something that happened recently. When tasted blind, Coeur d'Arras can easily be mistaken for Maroilles, the recipes are so close. It is closer-textured, because, being smaller, it ripens more quickly. This little heart is as meltingly soft as you could possibly wish and utterly irresistible.

Family
Munster
Country
France
Area of origin
Artois
Animal species
Cow
Milk
Pasteurized
Product
Cottage industry
Optimum ripening
1 month

Crayeux de Roncq

Northern France

Cow's milk

Crayeux de Roncq (or Carré du Vinage when less ripened) gets its name from a little town about 30 kilometres (18 miles) from Lille. A farmhouse product made from raw milk, it was created in 1985 by Thérèse-Marie Couvreur, in conjunction with Philippe Olivier, retailer at Boulogne-sur-Mer. This energetic farmer's daughter, who strayed into office work for a while, hoped to produce a 'Maroilles that was more delicate than the farmhouse products of the time, but with more flavour than the industrially made ones'. After two or three years of trying, she achieved in making her mark and finding the right formula, as is proved by the success her Crayeux enjoys far beyond the boundaries of its northern home. This thick cheese, with its orange rind and strong smell, needs to be ripened for six weeks before its initial chalky texture merges and softens. It needs frequent washing in salt water and beer (unpasteurized *de l'Angelus*). Thérèse is happy to welcome visitors to her workshop, specially fitted with a gallery and a shop selling produce of the local area.

Family
Munster

Country
France

Area of origin
Flanders

Animal species
Cow

Milk
Raw

Product
Farmhouse

Optimum ripening
2 months

Dauphin
Northern France
Cow's milk

Family
Munster
Country
France
Area of origin
Flanders
Animal species
Cow
Milk
Raw or pasteurized
Product
Cottage industry
or industrial
Optimum ripening
4 months

A derivative of Maroilles, Dauphin (dolphin) is made in a region that has nothing of the maritime about it. Its shape is a nod in the direction of history. When Louis XIV went to the Hainaut province to claim the territories ceded to him under the terms of the Treaty of Nijmegen, his hosts prepared a very out-of-the-ordinary cheese for him. It was a Maroilles – the pride of the local area – flavoured with fresh herbs. It was greatly enjoyed by the royal cortège, which included the King's heir – the Dauphin. This occasion made the cheese's reputation and it was duly given the name – and the shape – of a dolphin. It is made from Maroilles that has been damaged in production and not presentable enough to be sold. The curd is kneaded with different herbs and spices (tarragon, parsley, cloves, pepper), and coloured with *rocou* (a Mexican plant used as a vegetable dye). Its composition is much the same as that of Boulette d'Avesnes. Dauphin is ripened for two to four months, long enough for the aromas and flavours of the different ingredients to merge perfectly.

Herve

Belgium

Cow's milk

Sandwiched between two big exporters of cheese – France and the Netherlands – Belgium is hard put to establish a foothold in the cheese community. Herve is its best-known product. It belongs in the wide category of soft-pressed, washed-rind cheeses which abound in the whole of north-west France. It is made in French-speaking Belgium and its origins go back at least to the time of Charles V. It was then called Remoudou, from *remoudre*, which is to say 're-milk', as in the case of Reblochon. The farmer used to wait until the proprietor was not watching before finishing milking. The very rich milk that resulted served to make small cheeses for domestic consumption. Herve is now made in a rectangular shape coated in a damp, orange rind. Washed regularly in beer, it has quite a strong flavour after two to three months of ripening, especially if it is made with raw milk, which is not always the case. It must not be confused with Plateau-de-Herve, a cylindrical cheese of the Saint-Paulin type, made in the same region, which is softer. The milk spirited away to make Herve was very probably originally ear-marked for making this cheese.

Family
Munster

Other name
Herve Kaas

Country
Belgium

Area of origin
Herve

Animal species
Cow

Milk
Raw or pasteurized

Product
Cottage industry
or industrial

Optimum ripening
3 months

Livarot
France (Southern Normandy)
Cow's milk

Family
Munster

Other name
Colonel

Country
France

Area of origin
Pays d'Auge

Animal species
Cow

Milk
Raw, partially pasteurized
or pasteurized

Product
Cottage industry
or industrial

Optimum ripening
2 months

Livarot was the premier Normandy cheese for a long time, before being dethroned by Camembert, which travels better. The area where it is produced is restricted to a very small zone within a radius of about 20 kilometres (12 miles) of the town of Livarot. It corresponds to the hills of the Pays d'Auge, the famous wooded landscape that typifies the countryside all the way from Épinal to Normandy, with its dovecotes beside houses and its apple trees in flower. You can recognize Livarot by the band of natural reeds (sedge) bound around its edge or, in their absence, paper bands. There are five of these bands around each Livarot, hence its nickname of 'Colonel' – alluding to the five rings that denote the rank of a French army colonel – but nowadays these are merely decorative. This member of the washed-rind cheese family has quite a clean-cut character when it is correctly ripened (about two months). Apart from its very definite flavour, the rich, full curd is delicate and supple and – when made from the milk of cows fed on fresh grass – a beautiful bright yellow colour. A matured Calvados would go wonderfully well with it. Its flavour is so distinctive that cheeses that – for whatever reason – have developed a flavour that resembles this proud Norman product, are often said to be 'Livaroted'.

Pont-l'Evêque

France (Southern Normandy)
Cow's milk

Seemingly cramped in its square box, which it has a tendency to overflow, Pont-l'Evêque is a generous cheese, like the rich Normandy pastures that it transforms to perfection. It comes from the Pays d'Auge, the prodigious farming region that also gave us Livarot and Camembert. Pont l'Evêque is the name of a little town between Deauville and Lisieux. The area covered by the appellation contains sixteen producers, half of whom produce farmhouse cheeses. There are two types of Pont l'Evêque, depending on the method chosen to mature them. The first is brushed regularly during ripening: the fine, light-coloured mould that grows on its rind takes on a pinkish-grey hue, with reddish streaks. The cheese has a characteristic nutty flavour. This type is the one most frequently sold in supermarkets, because of its excellent keeping qualities. The second – which I prefer – is washed regularly in salt water during its time in the cellar. This encourages the development of 'red' ferment that gives an orange tint to the rind and a firmer texture. A good Pont l'Evêque only comes to its full richness after five or six weeks but, as your taste buds will tell you, it is well worth the wait!

Family
Munster
Country
France
Area of origin
Normandy
Animal species
Cow
Milk
Raw, partially pasteurized or pasteurized
Product
Farmhouse, cottage industry or industrial
Optimum ripening
2 months

Vieux-Boulogne

Northern France

Cow's milk

The north-western region of France is the home of soft-pressed and washed-rind cheeses, and Philippe Olivier, my fellow cheese-*affineur*, has become their harbinger. He was behind the production of Vieux-Boulogne. He and a young cheese-maker made many preliminary attempts and for the first time, in 1982, he introduced this cheese, which is similar in appearance to a Pont-l'Evèque. Since then, three small producers have begun making Vieux-Boulogne (the 'Vieux-' name-form is common in the north, where there is also a Vieux-Lille and a Vieux-Gris-de Lille). The cows are pastured between Blanc-Nez and Gris-Nez, where the frequent strong winds blow the damp, salty air onto the grass and give rise to a very specific kind of fungal growth. The lightly pressed curd is very close-textured and permits fermentation holes to form, and the rind is washed with Saint-Léonard beer – an original touch. The ripening period is two months on average. I should stress that here we have a cheese with both character and presence – a happy development that demonstrates the vitality of the farming world. While traditional products, often dating from a long way back, are disappearing regularly, others are being brought forward and forming new traditions.

Family
Munster
Country
France
Area of origin
Boulogne region
Animal species
Cow
Milk
Raw
Product
Cottage industry
Optimum ripening
2 months

Making the La Graine Johe Munster, near the Col du Bonhomme. The utensils used in the moulding have not changed in more than half a century.

The Pérail family
and related cheeses

These ewe's milk cheeses are quite mildly flavoured
for the most part. Covered with a white bloom,
they become creamy as they ripen.

Milk: R = raw, PP = partially pasteurized, P = pasteurized. Product: F = farmhouse, C = cottage industry, I = industrial.

Cheese	Other names	Country/Area of origin	Animal	Milk	Product	Label	Ripening
Emlett		🇬🇧 Avon	🐑	R	C		6 weeks
Flower Mary		🇬🇧 Sussex	🐑	R	C		6 weeks
Little Rydings		🇬🇧 Avon	🐑	R	C		2 months
Weisser prinz		▬	🐑	P	I		1 month
Berger plat		🇫🇷 Bresse	🐑	R	F		1 month
Brebiou		🇫🇷 Jurançon	🐑	P	I		2 weeks
Brebis de Meyrueis		🇫🇷 Languedoc-Roussillon – Corsica	🐑	R	F		3 weeks
Caldegousse		🇫🇷 Aveyron	🐑	R	C		15 days
Castagniccia		🇫🇷 Corsica	🐑	R	C		1 month
Fedo		🇫🇷 Provence	🐑	R	C		2 weeks
Fromageon fermier		🇫🇷 Rouergue	🐐🐑	R	F		2 weeks
Gayrie, La		🇫🇷 Rouergue	🐑	R	F		6 weeks
Lacandou		🇫🇷 Rouergue	🐑	R	C		3 weeks
Nabouly d'en haut		🇫🇷 Pyrenees	🐑	R	F		3 weeks
Notle		🇫🇷 Touraine	🐑	R	C		3 weeks
Pérail		🇫🇷 Rouergue	🐑	R	F, C		3 weeks
Tomme de brebis d'Arles		🇫🇷 Camargue	🐑	R	F		3 weeks
Vieux corse		🇫🇷 Northern Corsica	🐑	R	C		3 months
Paglietta		🇮🇹 Piedmont	🐄	P	C		1 month
Azeitão		🇵🇹 Extremadura	🐑	R	I	AOC-AOP	1 month

Pérail

France (Midi-Pyrenees)
Ewe's milk

This succulent little disc-shaped cheese made from ewe's milk has taken centuries to emerge from the shadow of the imposing local star, Roquefort. In the past, Pérail was only made during that period when Roquefort was out of production – that is to say during the second half of the year, when the ewes are still giving milk but in lesser quantities. This milk was particularly rich and went to make Pérail. This cheese now has a life of its own and is made all the year round. One of the prime movers in its emancipation is Jean-François Dombre, cheese-maker-*affineur* and producer of Pérail des Cabasses who fortunately, thirty years ago, declined an opportunity to leave the area and become a government official in Paris. The milk is collected in a wide area that runs from the Grands Causses to the Mediterranean *garrigues*, via the foothills of the Cevennes mountains, traditional sheep-farming lands. Ewe's milk is generally used to make either Tommes or Roquefort. In Pérail it shows a more restrained, subtle side to its character; made into this attractive little cheese, it is a real delicacy.

Family
Pérail
Country
France
Area of origin
Rouergue
Animal species
Ewe
Milk
Raw
Product
Farmhouse or cottage industry
Optimum ripening
3 weeks

The Rotolo family
and related cheeses

These ewe's milk cheeses have a rather stronger flavour than those belonging to the Pérail family; this is caused by frequent washing in the ripening cellars. They, too, readily take on a creamy texture.

Milk: R = raw, PP = partially pasteurized, P = pasteurized. Product: F = farmhouse, C = cottage industry, I = industrial.

Cheese	Other names	Country/Area of origin	Animal	Milk	Product	Label	Ripening
Herriot Farmhouse		Yorkshire		P	F		3 months
Brebichon de Haute-Provence		Haute-Provence		R	F		5 weeks
Brebis du Lochois		Touraine		R	F		1 month
Caussedou		Quercy		R	F		1 month
Fium' orbo		Corsica		R	F, C		2 months
Moularen		Provence		R	F		1 month
Niolo		Corsica – Plateau de Niolo		R	F		3 months
Rotolo		Corsica		R	F		6 months
U rustinu		Northern Corsica		R	F, C		4 months

Rotolo

France (Corsica)
Ewe's milk

Rotolo is derived from a traditional Corsican cheese called *Bastelicaccia*, which I, personally, ripen for much longer than normal. It is named after a village near Porticcio, where I met two people, Jean-François Brunelli and his mother Madeleine (*La Mamma*), who have been making *Brocciu* for decades. If you should be in the area, you might be lucky enough to watch her moulding her cheeses beneath the shade of the olive trees. The family has been producing them since 1891! The farm's pastures border the sea and about 120 ewes roam freely there. The cheeses are made in the morning, with the morning's milk together with that of the night before, which has been kept cool. The milk is made into Bastelicaccia, an unpressed, soft-curd cheese, cylindrical in shape (from 12 to 14 centimetres (4.7 to 5.4 inches) in diameter, and 4 to 5 centimetres (1.5 to 2 inches) thick), and the whey left from it is turned into Brocciu. While Brocciu is sold all over Continental France, either fresh or matured, Bastelicaccia is hardly known outside Corsica. No doubt this is because it is eaten too fresh and so does not have the time to reveal its very original flavour. I have chosen, therefore, with Jean-François' agreement, to ripen his Bastelicaccia for a minimum of six months and up to a year, and to market it under the name of Rotolo. I think he too was surprised at the resulting flavour.

Family
Rotolo

Country
France

Area of origin
Corsica

Animal species
Ewe

Milk
Raw

Product
Farmhouse

Optimum ripening
6 months

The Vacherin family
and related cheeses

A speciality of Franco-Swiss origin, this category offers rich, generous cheeses that need to be wrapped and kept in boxes so that their creamy curd does not collapse.

Milk: R = raw, PP = partially pasteurized, P = pasteurized. Product: F = farmhouse, C = cottage industry, I = industrial.

Cheese	Other names	Country/Area of origin	Animal	Milk	Product	Label	Ripening
Vacherin Chaput		Montérégie		R	F		1 month
Cabri ariégeois		Comté de Foix		R	C		6 weeks
Mont-d'or	Vacherin du Haut-Doubs	Doubs		R	C, I	AOC-AOP	1 month
Vacherin d'Abondance		Savoy – Vallée d'Abondance		R	F		1 month
Vacherin des Aillons		Bauges		R	F		3 months
Vacherin des Bauges		Bauges		R	F		2 months
Vacherin mont-d'or	Mont-d'or de Joux	Swiss Jura		R, P	C		1 month

Mont d'Or

France (Franche-Comté)
Cow's milk

Each autumn, the return of Mont d'Or (or Vacherin in the high areas of the Doubs) celebrates the affinity between wood and cheese. This is no mere coincidence. Direct contact with its restricting box and the spruce bands that encircle it, impregnate Mont d'Or with a soft, balsamic aroma. This is, above all, a winter cheese, and only in demand when the temperature plummets. Indeed, originally it was only made from All Saints' Day to Easter. Nowadays it makes its appearance around the middle of August, gives generously of itself throughout the winter and bows out at the beginning of spring (March 30th). A dozen cheese dairies make Mont d'Or but, since seasonal production is uneconomic, they all make Compté as well, and even Morbier and Raclette. However, for all of them Mont d'Or is the most exigent and the most delicate. It is very labour intensive, needing binding, brushing, washing, turning and boxing. The cheeses stay in the cellar for at least three weeks. I keep mine for twice that length of time; by then the rind has crinkled and the curd is creamy. To my customers I recommend removing the top rind and eating the cheese with a spoon. Such a treat! One can well understand why it is so widely copied.

Family
Vacherin
Other name
Vacherin du Haut-Doubs
Country
France
Area of origin
Doubs
Animal species
Cow
Milk
Raw
Product
Cottage industry
or industrial
Optimum ripening
1 month

The Saint-Nectaire family
and related cheeses

The curd for these cow's milk cheeses is lightly pressed in the course of production. During ripening, which takes place in a damp environment, their quite close texture softens and becomes creamy.

Milk: R = raw, PP = partially pasteurized, P = pasteurized. Product: F = farmhouse, C = cottage industry, I = industrial.

Cheese	Other names	Country/Area of origin	Animal	Milk	Product	Label	Ripening
Northumberland		Northumberland		P	F		3 months
Spenwood		Berkshire		R	C		6 months
Torville		Somerset		R	F		2 months
Beauvoorde				P	C		2 months
Victor et Berthold		Lanaudière		R	C		3 months
Bethmale	Oustet	Ariège – Comté de Foix		R, P	C, I		6 months
Chambérat		Bourbonnais		R, PP	F, C		3 months
Colombière		Alps		R	C		3 months
Doux de montagne		Haute-Garonne, Ariège		R	F		4 months
E bamalou		Ariège – Comté de Foix		R	C		2 months
Fourme de Rochefort		Auvergne		R	F		3 months
Fromage de Lège		Central Pyrenees		R	F		6 months
Fromage du pic de la Calabasse		Comté de Foix		R	F		3 months
Montagnard, Le		Franche-Comté		R	C		2 months
Moulis		Pyrenees – Comté de Foix		R	C		3 months
Murol		Auvergne		P	I		2 months
Murolait	Trou de Murol	Auvergne		P	I		15 days
Pavin		Auvergne		P	I		2 months
Petit pardou, Le		Béarn		R	C		2 months
Phébus		Comté de Foix		R	C		3 months
Reblochon		Aravis		R	F, C, I	AOC-AOP	6 weeks
Rogallais		Comté de Foix		R	C		2 months

Cheese	Other names	Country/Area of origin	Animal	Milk	Product	Label	Ripening
Saint-nectaire		Auvergne		R, PP, P	F, C, I	AOC-AOP	3 months
Savaron		Auvergne		P	C		2 months
Tomme de montagne des Vosges		Vosges		R	F		3 months
Toupin		Northern Savoy		R	C		4 months
Durrus		Cork		R	C		3 months
Gubbeen		Cork		P	F		3 months
Milleens		Cork		R	F		4 months
Branzi		Lombardy		R, P	C		6 months
Caerphilly		Wales		R, PP, P	F		2 months
Tournagus		Wales		R	C		3 months
Wedmore		Wales		R	C		1 month

Chambérat
France (Auvergne)
Cow's milk

Made in the Bourbonnais region, this cheese disappeared in the 1960s, when the last woman farmer gave up production. It was re-launched in 1989 by Yves Adrian, of the Du Chalet cheese dairy at Domérat. Based on information gleaned from the local people, he set about exhuming this quite distinctive, chunky, creamy cheese. Its reddish rind, covered with a fine white film, is reminiscent of Reblochon but its curd is more like that of a Saint-Nectaire. The dairy has since encouraged four farmhouse producers to join in the Chambérat venture by supplying them with materials, advice on making the cheese and technical assistance. These farmers now account for more than half of the cheeses produced. This is sufficient to arouse hopes for an AOC, the area of which would correspond to the historic Combraille – a region of plateaux and deep coombs taking in Puy-de-Dôme, Allier and Creuse. Chambérat could then consider aiming at larger markets than its own immediate area, where it seems to be greatly appreciated.

Family
Saint-Nectaire
Country
France
Area of origin
Bourbonnais
Animal species
Cow
Milk
Raw or partially pasteurized
Product
Farmhouse or cottage industry
Optimum ripening
3 months

Phébus

France (Midi-Pyrenees)
Cow's milk

Perched beneath the Col del Fach, Philippe Garros,
goat breeder and producer of an original and very
seductive Cabri Ariégeois, was not slow to notice
the immense cheese-making potential of the milk
produced by a neighbouring farmer, who raises
thirty or so *Brunes des Alpes* – an Alpine breed,
brown in colour – using traditional methods, and
who used to sell all his milk to a co-operative. The milk
from these cows is highly regarded by cheese producers for
its rich protein content, and since 1999, Philippe now buys a
part of the yield and makes it into this large Tomme, which
is similar to a Bethmale. A single cheese needs 50 to 55 litres
(88 to 96 pints) of milk. He has called his cheese 'Phébus' in
honour of a local mediaeval figure, the Chevalier Gaston
Phébus. Philippe Garros has espoused a tradition and
rediscovered a cheese from the past. The rind is, as it was
then, *cendré* – powdered with vegetable charcoal – after
an ideal ripening period of four months, during which time
it is washed regularly. The texture of the cheese is quite
supple, almost melting, and it exudes rich, very voluptuous,
fruity aromas.

Family
Saint-Nectaire
Country
France
Area of origin
Comté de Foix
Animal species
Cow
Milk
Raw
Product
Cottage industry
Optimum ripening
3 months

Reblochon

France (Rhône-Alpes)
Cow's milk

Centred on the Thônes valley in the Aravis mountain chain, the Reblochon *terroir* covers the eastern part of Haute-Savoie and the north of Savoie. The altitude is never less than 500 metres (1600 feet). More than 200 farmers, together with numerous cheese dairies, ensure the continued vitality of this cheese, a delicious treat once it has become creamy, glossy and very aromatic. I recommend a visit to the market at Grand-Bornand, which is held every Wednesday; at the edge of the traditional market, thirty or so people sell their wares alongside the church, from capacious pine chests inside which are 'white' Reblochons, pale and slightly frothy, from one to two weeks old; the *affineurs* take weekly delivery of the cheeses produced by farmers in the area. Among them is Joseph Paccard from Manigod, who knows just how to bring out the aromatic potential of these cheeses without rushing them, simply by washing them in salt water (which causes the rind to turn pinkish orange). Look at the rind; if it is flat the cheese will still be quite firm, whereas if it is domed then the cheese will be soft and creamy. It needs five or six weeks of ripening to make a really good Reblochon. As it is quite fragile once opened, it should be eaten fairly quickly.

Family
Saint-Nectaire
Country
France
Area of origin
Aravis
Animal species
Cow
Milk
Raw
Product
Farmhouse, cottage industry or industrial
Optimum ripening
6 weeks

It takes up to six weeks to bring Reblochon cheeses to perfection.

Saint-Nectaire

France (Auvergne)

Cow's milk

Family

Saint-Nectaire

Country

France

Area of origin

Auvergne

Animal species

Cow

Milk

Raw, partially pasteurized
or pasteurized

Product

Farmhouse, cottage
industry or industrial

Optimum ripening

3 months

Saint-Nectaire is a rustic cheese with a good smell of earth and humus. Beneath its rind – sometimes covered with yellowish or reddish mould – the supple, soft curd combines delicacy with a full flavour. It is sophisticated and distinguished. It once graced the table of Louis XIV, the Sun King, having been taken there around 1655 by Henri de la Ferté-Senneterre, Marshal of France, who gave it its name. Made in the Massif du Mont-Dore, in central Auvergne, its *terroir* is made up of volcanic earth covered by rich grassland. While the bulk of production nowadays is industrial, some five hundred farmhouse cheesemakers ensure its vitality. Until 1990, my friend Philippe Jaubert, *affineur*, whose business was created by his grandfather in 1908, used the ancient, traditional method of ripening on rye straw laid straight on the earth floor. In natural cellars that are a hundred and fifty years old, he ripened the cheeses from six or seven producers, some of whom still take their herds to the high pastures in summer. Saint-Nectaire is made with either a greyish, brushed rind, like those made by farmers in the mountains, or a washed rind with an orange tinge, like the ones made in the lowlands. Each one has its adherents.

The Tomme de Savoie family
and related cheeses

These cheeses are made in a very similar way to Saint-Nectaire. The main difference is in the ripening, the rind of the Tomme being simply brushed. Generally speaking it is greyish and the curd is drier.

Milk: R = raw, PP = partially pasteurized, P = pasteurized. Product: F = farmhouse, C = cottage industry, I = industrial.

Cheese	Other names	Country/Area of origin	Animal	Milk	Product	Label	Ripening
Coquetdale		Northumberland	cow	P	F		3 months
Cotherstone		Durham	cow	R	C		3 months
Menallack farmhouse		Cornwall	cow	R	C		6 months
Saint-basile		Quebec region	cow	R	F		3 months
Cantabria		Santander	cow	P	C, I	AOC-AOP	6 months
Formatge de la Selva		Catalonia	cow	R, P	C		4 months
Queso ahumado		Navarre	cow, goat, sheep	R	C		6 months
Bargkass		Vosges	cow	R, PP	F		2 months
Bourricot		Auvergne	cow	P	I		2 months
Esbareich		Central Pyrenees	cow	R	F		3 months
Fouchtra		Cantal	cow	R	F, C		6 months
Fromage de Poubeau		Central Pyrenees	cow	R	C		3 months
Fromage de vache brûlé		Basque country	cow	R	C		3 months
Lou magré		Gascony	cow	R	C		3 months
Montségur		Pyrenees	cow	P	I		3 months
Persillé du Semnoz		Savoy	cow, goat	R	F		2 months
Petite tomme beulet		Northern Savoy	cow	P	I		6 weeks
Pyrénées de vache		Pyrenees	cow	P	I		3 months
Tome des Bauges		Bauges	cow	R	F, C		2 months
Tomette de Yenne		Rhône-Alps	cow	R	C		2 months
Tomme au marc de raisin		Savoy region	cow	R	C		2 months
Tomme d'alpage de la Vanoise		Savoy	cow	R	C		3 months
Tomme d'Auvergne		Auvergne	cow	R, P	C		2 months
Tomme de Bonneval		Haute-Maurienne	cow	R	C, I		2 months
Tomme de chèvre de la vallée de Novel		Savoy	goat	R	F		6 months
Tomme de l'Aveyron		Larzac	cow	R	F		3 months
Tomme de la Frasse		Savoy	cow	R	F		6 months

Cheese	Other names	Country/Area of origin	Animal	Milk	Product	Label	Ripening
Tomme de Lomagne		Gascony	cow	R	C		2 months
Tomme de Lullin		Savoy	cow	R	C		6 months
Tomme de ménage	Boudane	Haute-Tarentaise	cow	R	F		3 months
Tomme de Morzine		Savoy	sheep	R	F		6 months
Tomme de Pont-Astier		Doubs	cow	R, P	C		2 months
Tomme de Savoie		Savoy region	cow	R, PP, P	F, C, I	IGP	4 months
Tomme de Thônes		Savoy – Chaîne des Aravis	cow	R	F		2 months
Tomme de Val-d'Isère		Savoy – Haute-Tarentaise	cow	R	F		2 months
Tomme des Allobroges		Savoy region	cow	R	F		3 months
Tomme des Allues		Savoy	cow	R, P	C		3 months
Tomme des Aravis		Savoy region	cow	R	F		3 months
Tomme du Beaujolais		Beaujolais	cow	P	C		2 months
Tomme du bougnat		Auvergne	cow	R	F		2 months
Tomme du Faucigny		Savoy	cow	R	F		5 months
Tomme du Mont-Cenis		Savoy	cow	R	F		3 months
Tomme du Pelvoux		Savoy	cow	R	C		3 months
Tomme du Revard		Savoy	cow	R, P	C		3 months
Tomme fermière des Lindarets		Savoy	cow	R	F		6 months
Tomme grise de Seyssel		Savoy	cow	R	C		6 months
Tomme le Gascon		Gascony	cow	R	C		2 months
Tommette de l'Aveyron		Rouergue	sheep	R	F		2 months
Vachard		Auvergne	cow	R	C		2 months
Bra		Piedmont	cow, goat, sheep	R, P	F, C	AOC-AOP	6 months
Raschera		Piedmont	cow, goat, sheep	R, P	F, C	AOC-AOP	3 months
Sora		Piedmont	cow, sheep	R, P	C		1 year
Toma brusca		Piedmont	cow	R, P	F, C		4 months
Toma del maccagno		Piedmont	cow	R, P	F, C		2 months
Toma di capra		Piedmont	cow	R, P	F, C		4 months
Toma di lanzo		Piedmont	cow	R, P	F, C		3 months
Toma piemontese		Piedmont	cow	R, P	C	AOC-AOP	4 months
Toma valle elvo		Piedmont	cow	R, P	F, C		3 months
Toma valsesia		Piedmont	cow	R, P	F, C		3 months
Valle d'Aosta fromadzo		Lombardy, Aosta valley	cow	R	C		9 months
Alvorca			cow, goat, sheep	R	C		6 months

Tome des Bauges

France (Rhône-Alpes)
Cow's milk

Even though urbanization is gradually invading the outer slopes, Les Bauges are still traditionally inhabited by mountain people. This is the home of the very best Tommes de Savoie – a cheese that mass-production is making increasingly commonplace. The award of an AOC – 'Tome des Bauges' – based on serious criteria, is a step in the right direction: only raw milk to be used, supplementary ferments banned, priority given to local breeds (Tarine or Abondance cows), use of curd pumps banned as too harsh, minimum ripening period of five weeks in the appellation zone, etc. The Tomes des Bauges that I offer my customers are matured for more than two months, prepared for me by Denis Provent who goes to collect them, sometimes from up on the high pastures, from Alfred, Dominique, Stéphane, René, François and the others, some of the twenty or so producers who ensure the continued vitality of this cheese. Like all the other Tommes, Tome des Bauges has a greyish rind, with a pronounced mushroom flavour, enclosing a fairly soft cheese. In summer, the rind is sometimes tinged with pink, and in winter with traces of sulphur-yellow. It can also be profoundly capricious, like all farmhouse cheeses.

Family
Tomme de Savoie
Country
France
Area of origin
Bauges
Animal species
Cow
Milk
Raw
Product
Farmhouse or
cottage industry
Optimum ripening
2 months

The Chevrotin family
and related cheeses

Characteristic of these goat's milk cheeses, of which there are a great many in the Alps, is the process of pressing the curd during production. They have a quite dense texture and a pronounced goat's milk flavour.

Milk: R = raw, PP = partially pasteurized, P = pasteurized. Product: F = farmhouse, C = cottage industry, I = industrial.

Cheese	Other names	Country/Area of origin	Animal	Milk	Product	Label	Ripening
Basing		Kent	goat	R	F		2 months
Loddiswel Avondale		Devon	goat	R	F		2 months
Ribblesdale		Yorkshire	goat	R	F		2 months
Ticklemore		Devon	goat	R	F, C		3 months
Vulscombe		Devon	goat	R	F		1 month
Wigmore		Berkshire	goat	R	F		2 months
Capra (Le)		Lanaudière	goat	R	F		1 month
Breña			goat	R	C		3 months
Garrotxa		Catalonia	goat	R, P	C		3 months
Ibores		Extremadura	goat	R	F, C		3 months
Queso del Montsec	Cendrat	Catalonia	goat	R	C		3 months
Queso majorero		Canaries	goat	R	F, C	AOC-AOP	2 months
Annot		Inland Nice region	goat	R	C		2 months
Asco		Northern Corsica	goat sheep	R	F		3 months
Aubisque		Pyrenees – Ossau valley	goat sheep	R	C		3 months
Cabrioulet	Tomme Loubières	Comté de Foix	goat	R	F		3 months
Caprinu		Corsica		R	C		6 months
Chèvre fermier des Pyrénées		Béarn-Gascony Midi-Pyrenees	goat	R	C		1 month
Chevrotin de Macôt		Savoy – Tarentaise	goat	R	F		2 months
Chevrotin de Montvalezan		Savoy – Tarentaise	goat	R	F		2 months
Chevrotin de Morzine		Savoy	goat	R	F		3 months
Chevrotin de Peizey-Nancroix		Savoy	goat	R	F		3 months
Chevrotin des Aravis		Northern Savoy – Aravis	goat	R	F		2 months
Chevrotin des Bauges		Bauges	goat	R	F		2 months

Cheese	Other names	Country/Area of origin	Animal	Milk	Product	Label	Ripening
Chevrotin du Mont-Cenis		Savoy		R	F		2 months
Figue		Périgord		R	C		3 weeks
Fort de la Platte		Briançon region		R	C		6 months
Grataron d'Arèches		Savoy		R	F		2 months
Grataron de Haute-Luce		Savoy		R	F		2 months
Lou pennol		Southern Quercy		R	F		3 months
Palouse des Aravis		Alps – Aravis		R	F		6 months
Pêchegros		Tarn		R	F, C		1 month
Sarteno		Corsica		R	F		3 months
Tome de chèvre de Gascogne		Gascony		R	F		2 months
Tome pressée		Provence		R	F		1 year
Tomme au muscadet		Loire region		R	C		6 months
Tomme de chèvre corse		Corsica		R	F		3 months
Tomme de chèvre de Belleville		Savoy – Tarentaise		R	F		2 months
Tomme de chèvre de la vallée de Morzine		Savoy		R	C		2 months
Tomme de chèvre de Provence		Provence		R	C		1 month
Tomme de chèvre Pays nantais		Nantes region		R	F		6 weeks
Tomme de Courchevel		Savoy		R	F		2 months
Tomme de Crest				R	F		2 months
Tomme de huit litres		Provence		R	F		6 months
Tomme de Vendée		Vendée		R	C		2 months
Tomme du Pays basque		Basque country		R	F		3 months
Tomme du Vercors		Vercors		R	F		2 months
Tomme fermière des Hautes-Vosges		Hautes-Vosges		P	C		3 months
Tomme mi-chèvre de Lécheron		Savoy		R	F		3 months
Tomme mi-chèvre des Bauges		Savoy		R	F		2 months
Tomme sainte-Cécile		Burgundy		R	F		6 months
Tommette mi-chèvre des Bauges		Bauges		R	F		2 months
Valdeblore		Inland Nice region		R	C		2 months
Kefalotyri				R	F, C		3 months
Croghan		Wexford		R	F		3 months
Gjetost				P	I		1 month

Chevrotin des Bauges

France (Rhône-Alpes)
Goat's milk

Family
Chevrotin
Country
France
Area of origin
Bauges
Animal species
Goat
Milk
Raw
Product
Farmhouse
Optimum ripening
2 months

This one has all the virtues! Chevrotin des Bauges, made always with full-flavoured milk from the mountains, exudes natural goodness with its thick, greyish rind and yellow or red growth of mould, according to season – even pink, in the summer. Four or five cheesemakers produce it at Les Bauges, a mountain region that forms a natural, well-defined entity between Annecy, Chambéry and Albertville, partly in Savoie and partly in Haute Savoie.

Les Bauges rises to an altitude of 2,200 metres (7,000 feet) and the villages are situated at between 600 and 1,100 metres (2,000 and 3,500 feet). This region, though basically cow's milk Tommes country, has been producing this goat's milk version for a long time now. A Chevrotin uses about six litres (ten pints) of milk and needs a good two months of ripening for its curd to soften. I leave this in the hands of Denis Provent, *affineur* at Chambéry, who knows every nook and cranny of the mountains. He works principally with a producer who has divided his herd into three groups to stagger the lactation periods and avoid spending long months out of production ... which frustrates the winter-sports enthusiasts who come to the area. Denis assures me that a bottle of Gamay from Savoy goes very well with Chevrotin. You should try it!

Grataron d'Arèches

France (Rhône-Alpes)
Goat's milk

Warning, cheese in the process of disappearing! Denis Provent, cheese-*affineur* at Chambéry, never stops reminding me: the last three producers of Grataron d'Arèches are already getting on in years and their holdings are too small to be of interest to a possible rescuer. It would be a damaging loss, for this very attractive product is quite unique. To the best of Denis's knowledge it is the only soft-pressed, washed-rind goat's milk cheese in the whole of the Alps. It is produced at an altitude of about 1,500 metres (5,000 feet), at the heart of Beaufortin, on a valley floor, and it has never been imitated outside that area. At the start of the twentieth century it was made in every house. The peasants washed it – probably to remove the 'cat's hair' (the grey mould characteristic of Tommes de Savoie), which becomes intrusive in very damp weather. In the summer, when there was an abundance of milk, the production of Tommes took over.

In the cellar, the cheese is regularly washed with a sponge soaked in saline. The rind slowly takes on an orange to ochre colour, and the texture is soft. It is reminiscent of Reblochon, but with the flavour of Tomme and a little extra touch of salt that makes it very good indeed.

Family
Chevrotin
Country
France
Area of origin
Savoy
Animal species
Goat
Milk
Raw
Product
Farmhouse
Optimum ripening
2 months

The Venaco family
and related cheeses

The soft, ewe's milk Tommes of this family are recognizable by their fine, full flavour, the strength of which depends on whether or not the rinds were washed during ripening.

Milk: R = raw, PP = partially pasteurized, P = pasteurized. Product: F = farmhouse, C = cottage industry, I = industrial.

Cheese	Other names	Country/Area of origin	Animal	Milk	Product	Label	Ripening
Aragón	Tronchón	Aragon		R	F		2 weeks
Penamellera		Asturias		R	F		2 months
A filetta	Fougère	Northern Corsica		R	C		1 month
Amou		South-West		R	F		4 months
Barousse		Pyrenees		R	F		2 months
Brebis de Bersend		Savoy		R	F		2 months
Brebis du pays de Grasse		Provence		R	F		2 months
Corsica		Corsica		R, P	C		1 month
Fromage des Pyrénées		Pyrenees		P	I		2 months
Galette du val de Dagne		Corbières		R	F		3 months
Napoléon		Corsica		R	C		6 weeks
Ourliou		Lot		P	C		2 months
Tomme de brebis		Savoy		R	F		1 month
Tomme de brebis de Haute-Provence		Haute-Provence		R	F		2 months
Tommette des Corbières		Corbières		R	F		2 months
Venaco		Northern Corsica		R	F		2 months
Orla		Cork		R	C		6 months
Caciotta toscana		Tuscany		P	C		3 weeks
Casciotta di Urbino		Marche		R, P	F	AOC-AOP	1 month
Marzolino		Tuscany		R, P	C		2 months
Queijo da Ovelha				R	C		2 months
Serpa		Alentejo		R	C	AOC-AOP	2 months
Serra da Estrela		Serra da Estrela		R	F, C	AOC-AOP	2 months

The Cheddar family
and related cheeses

Undoubtedly brought by the Romans to Britain, following their passage through Cantal, the recipe for Cheddar – which notably involves breaking up the curd, resulting in an uneven texture – is now used universally.

Milk: R = raw, PP = partially pasteurized, P = pasteurized. Product: F = farmhouse, C = cottage industry, I = industrial.

Cheese	Other names	Country/Area of origin	Animal	Milk	Product	Label	Ripening
Buffalo		🇬🇧 Hereford-Worcester	🐄	R	C		3 months
Cheddar		🇬🇧 Somerset	🐄	R, PP, P	F, I	AOC-AOP	1 year
Cheshire	Chester	🇬🇧 Cheshire	🐄	R, P	F, C, I		3 months
Cornish Yarg		🇬🇧 Cornwall	🐄	P	C		2 months
Costwold		🇬🇧	🐄	P	I		4 months
Denhay Dorset drum		🇬🇧 Dorset	🐄	P	F		2 months
Derby		🇬🇧 Derbyshire	🐄	P	I		4 months
Devon garland		🇬🇧 Devon	🐄	R	C		2 months
Double Gloucester		🇬🇧 Gloucestershire	🐄	R, P	F, C, I		6 months
Double Worcester		🇬🇧 Worcestershire	🐄	R	F		9 months
Gospel green		🇬🇧 Surrey	🐄	R	F		3 months
Hereford hop		🇬🇧 Gloucestershire	🐄	P	F, C		4 months
Lancashire		🇬🇧 Lancashire	🐄	R, P	F, C, I		6 months
Leicester	Red Leicester	🇬🇧 Leicestershire	🐄	P	I		6 months
Lincolnshire poacher		🇬🇧 Lincolnshire	🐄	R	C		6 months
Sage Derby		🇬🇧 Derbyshire	🐄	P	I		1 year
Sage Lancashire		🇬🇧	🐄	R, P	C, I		4 months
Single Gloucester		🇬🇧 Gloucestershire	🐄	R, P	F, C, I	AOC-AOP	9 months
Staffordshire organic		🇬🇧 Staffordshire	🐄	R	F		4 months
Swaledale		🇬🇧 Yorkshire	🐄 🐐	P	F	AOC-AOP	3 months
Wellington		🇬🇧 Berkshire	🐄	R	C		2 months
Wensleydale	White Wensleydale – White cheese	🇬🇧 Yorkshire	🐄	P	C, I		6 months
Cheedam		🇦🇺	🐄	P	I		1 year
Pyengana cheddar		🇦🇺 Tasmania	🐄	P	F		18 months
Cheddar l'ancêtre		🇨🇦 Bois-Francs	🐄	R	C		3 months

Cheese	Other names	Country/Area of origin	Animal	Milk	Product	Label	Ripening
Aran		🏴	🐄	R	C		1 year
Dunlop		🏴 Ayrshire	🐄	R	C, I		1 year
Gowrie		🏴 Perthshire	🐄	P	C		4 months
Isle of Mull		🏴 Isle of Mull	🐄	R	C		6 months
Lairobell		🏴 Orkney	🐄	R	C		6 months
Loch Arthur Farmhouse		🏴 Dumfries-Galloway	🐄	R	C		1 year
Orkney		🏴 Orkney	🐄	P	C		1 year
Scottish farmhouse cheddar		🏴	🐄	R	C		1 year
Cheddar de Shelburne		🇺🇸	🐄	R	C		1 year
Colby crowley		🇺🇸 Wisconsin-Vermont	🐄	P	I		6 months
Grafton cheddar		🇺🇸 Vermont	🐄	R	C		1 year
Longhorn		🇺🇸	🐄	P	I		6 months
Monterey	Monterey jack – Jack-bear flag	🇺🇸 California	🐄	P	I		10 months
Cantal	Fourme du Cantal	🇫🇷 Cantal	🐄	R, PP, P	F, C, I	AOC-AOP	1 year
Laguiole		🇫🇷 Aubrac (Aveyron, Cantal, Lozère)	🐄	R	C	AOC-AOP	18 months
Salers	Fourme de Salers – Cantal salers	🇫🇷 Cantal	🐄	R	F	AOC-AOP	18 months
Lavistown		🇮🇪 Kilkenny	🐄	R	C		3 months
Llanboidy		🏴 Pembrokeshire	🐄	R	F		6 months
Llangloffan farmhouse		🏴 Pembrokeshire	🐄	R	C		6 months
Tyn crug		🏴 Cardiganshire	🐄	R	C		6 months

Sage Derby
United Kingdom (England)
Cow's milk

A close relative of Cheddar, this sage version is the best-known of the Derby cheeses. The herbs, together with other flavourings, are incorporated at a very early stage, mixed directly into the curd in the course of moulding. The resulting cheese is marbled with green. Some cheese dairies add the herbs in a different way that produces a layered cheese, rather like a vanilla slice. To help in sorting and identifying the cheeses, they either carry a reproduction of a sage leaf on the rind or are coated with green paraffin wax. This cheese is primarily sold at Christmas time. Its flavour is much more subtle than its somewhat garish colour might lead one to expect. This genuine curiosity demonstrates how extremely accommodating cow's milk is (such a combination is unthinkable for goat's or ewe's milk) and how strongly the idiosyncrasies of the British character are reflected in culinary matters. Other bizarre combinations include Wensleydale with mint, apricots, ginger or bilberries, or Cheddar with onions and chives. This traditional love of spiced food was fuelled by the widely ranging conquests made by this great nation of travellers and traders.

Family
Cheddar
Country
England
Area of origin
Derbyshire
Animal species
Cow
Milk
Pasteurized
Product
Industrial
Optimum ripening
4 months

Laguiole

France (Auvergne)

Cow's milk

Family
Cheddar
Country
France
Area of origin
Aubrac (Aveyron, Cantal, Lozère)
Animal species
Cow
Milk
Raw
Product
Cottage industry
Optimum ripening
18 months

The high basalt plateaux of Aubrac, where this cheese is made, have imbued Laguiole with a primitive, mineral character, somewhat brusque in the first instance. But as it melts on the tongue it releases warm aromas of dried fruit, roast coffee beans, butter. Originally it was only made in the summer, when the cows – of the Aubrac breed – were up in the high pastures. Wars and the rural exodus almost sounded the death-knell of this magnificent cheese, but it was saved in 1960 by the cheese co-operative, Jeune Montagne. André Valadier, chairman of the company for the last forty years, was one of the principal architects of its rebirth. Since 1976, thanks to its commercial viability, Laguiole can now be made the whole year round. The area where it is produced rises from an altitude of 600 metres to 1,400 metres (2,000 feet to 4,500 feet). The abundant permanent grassland guarantees the presence of the very specific micro-organisms that undoubtedly contribute to the unique nature of this cheese. One Laguiole cheese needs 300 to 400 litres (500 to 700 pints) of milk. It must be ripened for at least four months, but this can be extended to a year or more. This is why one can find excellent Laguiole at any time of the year, including winter. Its irregular curd gradually takes on a slightly melting texture. A programme is under way to bring back the attractive local Aubrac breed of cows, with their almost flirtatious black-rimmed eyes.

Making Laguiole in the *buron* (workplace) at Carmejane. It requires a number of different operations to produce this treasure of the Aubrac Plateaux.

Salers
France (Auvergne)
Cow's milk

A clean, dominant acidity and a touch of bitterness –
Salers is not always very approachable, as is
indicated by its thick, rough rind. Austere
and rugged, it loses its reserve as it warms
up on the palate, offering rich, very full and
splendidly complex aromas of dried fruit
and butter. A fiery temperament, and well
justified! It must be made only from raw milk,
between May 1st and October 31st, at an altitude
of more than 850 metres (3,000 feet). It is definitely
not the kind of product sold in supermarkets. Its appellation
zone is restricted to Cantal and a few cantons bordering it.
It is produced exclusively by a hundred or so farms. From
his ring-side position at Saint-Flour, my brother Alain, a
retailer, always dreads the period from June to July when
he finds it difficult to bridge the gap between the previous
summer's excellent cheeses which have spent the winter in
the cellars, and those of the new season, which only reach
their best at the end of July. Contrary to popular belief,
Salers is rarely made from cows of the Salers breed,
recognizable by their lyre-shaped horns and their mahogany
colour; these animals are mainly bred for their famous beef.

Family
Cheddar
Other names
Fourme de Salers,
Cantal Salers
Country
France
Area of origin
Cantal
Animal species
Cow
Milk
Raw
Product
Farmhouse
Optimum ripening
18 months

The Gouda family
and related cheeses

Those great travellers, the Dutch, invented these pressed-curd cheeses, often coated with a protective paraffin-wax crust, which stack perfectly into the holds of ships without sustaining damage.

Milk: R = raw, PP = partially pasteurized, P = pasteurized. Product: F = farmhouse, C = cottage industry, I = industrial.

Cheese	Other names	Country/Area of origin	Animal	Milk	Product	Label	Ripening
Bianco				P	I		2 months
Deutsche trappistenkäse				P	I		2 months
Geheimratskäse				P	I		1 month
Geltinger		Schleswig-Holstein		P	I		3 months
Gouda allemand	Deutscher gouda			P	I		6 months
Schwäbischer landkäse				P	I		2 months
Steppe				P	I		6 months
Tilsit		Lithuania		P	I		3 months
Tollenser		Eastern Germany		P	I		2 months
Vitadam				P	I		1 month
Wilster marschkäse	Wilstermarsch	Holstein		P	I		3 months
Coverdale		Yorkshire		P	C		2 months
Curworthy		Devon		C	C		4 months
Steirischer bauernkäse				P	C		2 months
Steirischer hirtenkäse				P	C		2 months
Esrom	Bütterkäse danois			P	I	IGP	3 months
Havarti	Tilsit danois			P	I		2 months
Maribo		Island of Lolland		P	I		4 months
Molbo				P	I		3 months
Bola				P	I		3 months
Mahón		Balearic islands		C, PP, P	F, C, I	AOC-AOP	1 year
San simón		Galicia		C	F, C		2 months
Brick		Wisconsin		P	I		2 months
Kesti				P	I		2 months
Kreivi				P	I		2 months
Lappi				P	I		3 months
Babybel				P	I		1 month
Bonbel				P	I		1 month
Gouda français				P	I		6 months

Cheese	Other names	Country/Area of origin	Animal	Milk	Product	Label	Ripening
Mimolette	Boule de Lille – Vieux lille	Nord		PP, P	C, I		2 years
Pavé de Roubaix		Nord		P	C		1 year
Baby gouda	Lunchies kaas			P	I		3 months
Boerenkaas		Southern Netherlands		R	F, C	AOC-AOP	1 year
Edam	Tête de maure – Manbollen – Katzenkopf – Tête de chat	Northern Netherlands		P	I	AOC-AOP	6 months
Friese nagelkaas				P	C, I		3 months
Friese Nelkenkaas		Friesland		P	I		3 months
Friesekaas	Frise	Friesland		P	I		3 months
Gouda	Goudse kaas	Southern Netherlands		P	F, C, I	AOC-AOP	6 months
Kernhem				P	I		2 months
Kruidenkaas				P	C, I		3 months
Kummel				P	I		3 months
Leidener	Leidsekaas-Leiden	Leiden		P	C, I		1 year
Mimolette	Commissiekaas			P	I		6 months
Minell				P	I		1 month
Nagelkaas				P	C, I		3 months
Pardano				P	I		1 month
Roomkaas				P	I		3 months
Coolea		Cork		R	C		1 year
Doolin		Waterford		P	C		3 months
Bel Paese		North		P	I		2 months
Italico				P	I		2 months
Edda				P	I		2 months
Nökkelost				P	I		3 months
Norvegia				P	I		3 months
Penbryn		Carmarthenshire		P	I		2 months
Teifi		Carmarthenshire		R	C		3 months
Flamengo				P	C, I		6 months
São Jorge		Azores		R	F, C	AOC-AOP	6 months
Ambrosia				P	I		3 months
Drabant				P	I		3 months
Gårda				P	I		3 months
Gräddost				P	I		2 months
Kryddal				P	I		2 months
Prästost				P	C, I		2 months
Sveciaost	Svecia			P	I	IGP	3 months

Mimolette

France
Cow's milk

Beware of misconceptions! Mimolette is almost unknown among the Dutch, who prefer to export it. Its adopted home, and perhaps even where it originated, is France. It is possible that the French were inspired by Dutch cheeses (egged on notably by Colbert, advisor to Louis XIV), but the cheese may have come into being much earlier, in the vast region of Flanders, which was neither French nor Dutch, but Spanish. But what does it matter? French Mimolette, like the Special Reserve one I get from the co-operative at Isigny, when ripened for up to two years gives off an irresistible smell of hazelnuts. By that time it is hard and crumbly. The *affineurs* regularly sound the cheeses with a mallet to keep track of any irregularities in their make-up, and brush them about once a month so that mites – acarids that abound on the surface without posing any danger to human health – do not nibble at the paste. The Dutch prefer to coat the cheeses in protective paraffin wax.

The colour of the paste came originally from a Mexican plant called *rocou* but nowadays cheesemakers use carotene. A little historical note: Mimolettes from Isigny are made with milk from mixed herds containing equal numbers of French cows (Normandes) and Dutch (Holsteins).

Family
Gouda
Other names
Boule de Lille, Vieux Lille
Country
France
Area of origin
Nord
Animal species
Cow
Milk
Partially pasteurized
or pasteurized
Product
Cottage industry
or industrial
Optimum ripening
2 years

The Trappiste family
and related cheeses

The recipe for these pressed-curd cheeses, of which the best-known name is that of Port-Salut, has been handed down over the centuries by monasteries and abbeys. They are often washed-rind cheeses but, on the whole, their flavour remains fairly mild.

Milk: R = raw, PP = partially pasteurized, P = pasteurized. Product: F = farmhouse, C = cottage industry, I = industrial.

Cheese	Other names	Country/Area of origin	Animal	Milk	Product	Label	Ripening
Bruder Basil		Bavaria		P	I		1 month
Butterkäse				P	I		2 months
Limbourg	Limburger			P	I		3 months
Steinbuscher				P	I		2 months
King river gold		Victoria		P	C		2 months
Trappistenkäse				P	I		2 months
Abbaye de Leffe				P	C		3 months
Brigand				P	I		2 months
Chimay		French-speaking Belgium		P	C		3 months
Loo véritable				P	I		2 months
Maredsous				P	C		3 months
Orval	Abbaye d'Orval	Belgian Ardennes		P	C	Monastic	1 month
Passendale		Flanders		P	I		2 months
Plateau de herve		Herve		P	C, I		3 months
Postel				P	C		3 months
Rubens		Flanders		R, P	F, C		2 months
Saint Andrews		Perthshire		R	C		2 months
Abbaye de Citeaux	Trappe de Cîteaux, Trappiste de Cîteaux	Burgundy		R	F, C	Monastic	2 months
Abbaye de la Coudre		Brittany		P	C		3 months
Abbaye de la Joie Notre-Dame		Brittany		R	F		2 months
Abbaye de Timadeuc		Morbihan		P	C		2 months
Beaumont		Savoy		R, P	I		2 months
Belval	Trappe de Belval	Flanders-Artois-Picardy		C	C		2 months
Bricquebec	Abbaye de Bricquebec, Trappe de Bricquebec	Cotentin		P	C		3 months

Cheese	Other names	Country/Area of origin	Animal	Milk	Product	Label	Ripening
Campénac		Brittany	🐄	P	C		2 months
Chambarand	Trappiste de Chambarand	Savoy	🐄	P	C		2 months
Entrammes	Port du salut – Trappiste d'Entrammes	Mayenne	🐄	R, P	I		2 months
Fleuron d'Artois		Nord	🐄	R, P	F		4 months
Fromage d'Hesdin		Artois	🐄	R	C		2 months
Galette de Frencq		Nord	🐄	R	F		3 months
Igny	Trappiste d'Igny	Champagne	🐄	R	C		3 months
Laval	Trappiste de Laval	Maine	🐄	R	C		3 months
Meilleraye		Brittany	🐄	P	C		3 months
Monts-des-Cats	Trappe de Bailleul	Nord – Mont-des-Cats	🐄	R	C	Monastic	3 months
Oelenberg		Alsace	🐄	P	C		2 months
Port-Salut		Mayenne-Maine	🐄	P	I		3 months
Saint-paulin		Brittany and Maine	🐄	P	I		2 months
Saint-winoc		Flanders	🐄	R	F		2 months
Tamié	Abbaye de Tamié	Bauges Mountains	🐄	R	C		2 months
Trappe (abbaye de la Coudre)		Maine	🐄	P	C		1 month
Trappe d'Échourgnac		Périgord	🐄	P	C		3 months
Troisvaux		Ternois	🐄	R	C		2 months
Crimlin			🐄	P	I		2 months
Cushlee			🐄	P	I		2 months
Ridder			🐄	P	I		2 months
Celtic promise		Carmarthenshire	🐄	R	C		2 months
Saint David's		Monmouthshire	🐄	P	C		2 months
Ridder			🐄	P	I		2 months

Orval

Belgium (Champagne-Ardenne)
Cow's milk

Shaped like a brick, this authentic Trappiste cheese is quite a bright orange colour (it is dyed with *rocou*), and its paste is as supple and soft as a comfortable pillow. Made from pasteurized milk, its flavour is very mild and, altogether, it is not lacking in sensuality. The monks of Orval themselves collect the milk, make the cheeses and ripen them, all within the confines of the abbey. The milk comes from local farms – the abbey has not had its own herd since 1960. The recipe used is that of Port-Salut and the cheeses are ripened for three weeks in damp cellars before being marketed. If you stay at the hotel run by the abbey, you might perhaps discover the produce that the monks keep for their own consumption – a round cheese which is ripened in a dry cellar for six months, with a much drier paste and a more pronounced flavour, carried by a good length on the palate. Perhaps one day they will market it. The abbey is not obsessed by quantity – it is content to produce one hundred or so tonnes a year.

Family
Trappiste
Other name
Abaye d'Orval
Country
Belgium
Area of origin
Belgian Ardennes
Animal species
Cow
Milk
Pasteurized
Product
Cottage industry
Optimum ripening
1 month

Troisvaux

France (Picardy)
Cow's milk

Monastic cheeses have made spectacular progress throughout Europe thanks to the system of sponsorship and solidarity set up between abbeys. Monks and nuns exchange the recipes and secrets of their cheese-making techniques. It is difficult to imagine this happening among the farming community, who are jealous of their know-how and often mistrustful of each other. Down the generations, this system – now losing its impetus – has flourished magnificently, giving rise to a vast heritage. Troisvaux is an excellent example of this; like Belval, this cheese is made by the monks of the abbey of Sainte-Marie du Mont-des-Cats and ripened by the Trappist nuns at the Cistercian abbey of Notre-Dame de Belval, created in 1893. Only a small amount is made, the intention being that of providing work for the congregation. Troisvaux is ripened for seven to eight weeks and regularly washed in beer, also made at the abbey, which gives it a dark colour and a fairly lively flavour that is unusual in a cheese of the Port-Salut type. The people of northern France like to eat it on bread and butter and dip it in coffee made with chicory. Personally I love it with a glass of good beer.

Family
Trappiste
Country
France
Area of origin
Ternois
Animal species
Cow
Milk
Raw
Product
Cottage industry
Optimum ripening
2 months

The Manchego family
and related cheeses

Hard Tommes made from ewe's milk are the great speciality of the Iberian Peninsula. They will easily keep for up to two years but only the best of them do not become piquant. On the opposite page: preparing the moulds for Manchego.

Milk: R = raw, PP = partially pasteurized, P = pasteurized. Product: F = farmhouse, C = cottage industry, I = industrial.

Cheese	Other names	Country/Area of origin	Animal	Milk	Product	Label	Ripening
Berkswell		Midlands	🐑	R	F		3 months
Duddleswell		Sussex	🐑	R	C		4 months
Friesla		Devon	🐑	P	F		3 months
Leafield		Oxfordshire	🐑	P	C		2 months
Malvern		Hereford-Worcester	🐑	R	C		4 months
Tala		Cornwall	🐑	R	F		6 months
Tyning		Avon	🐑	R	F		1 year
Cairnsmore		Dumfries-Galloway	🐑	R	C		1 year
Aralar		Basque country	🐑	R	C, I		6 months
Castellano		Castille-Leon	🐑	R	F, C, I		6 months
Gorbea		Basque country	🐑	R	C, I		6 months
Grazamela		Cadiz region	🐑	R, P	C, I		6 months
Idiazábal		Basque country – Navarre	🐑	R	F, C	AOC-AOP	6 months
Manchego		La Mancha	🐑	R, P	F, C, I	AOC-AOP	1 year
Manchego en aceite		La Mancha	🐑	R, P	C, I		6 months
Orduña		Basque country	🐑	R	C, I		6 months
Oropesa de Tolède		Toledo region	🐑	R, P	C, I		6 months
Pedroches de Cordoue		Cordoba region	🐑	R, P	C, I		6 months
Queso iberico		Centre	🐑🐄🐐	P	C, I		4 months
Roncal		Navarre	🐑	R	F, C, I	AOC-AOP	1 year
Serena		Andalusia-Cordoba	🐑	R, P	C, I	AOC-AOP	6 months
Sierra de zuheros		Extremadura	🐑	R, P	F, C		6 months
Urbasa		Basque country	🐑	R	C, I		6 months
Urbia		Basque country	🐑	R	C, I		6 months
Zamorano		Castille-Léon	🐑	R	C	AOC-AOP	6 months
Abbaye de Belloc		Basque country	🐑	P	C, I		6 months
Ardi-gasna	Iraty	Basque country	🐑	R	F		18 months
Arnéguy		Pyrenees	🐑	R	C		6 months

Cheese	Other names	Country/Area of origin	Animal	Milk	Product	Label	Ripening
Aulus		Ariège		R	F		6 months
Cayolar		Basque country		R	C		6 months
Cierp de Luchon		Ariège		R	F		6 months
Etorki		South-West		P	I		2 months
Laruns		Pyrenees		R	C		6 months
Lavort	Médiéval	Auvergne		R	F		3 months
Matocq		Pyrenees		R	C		6 months
Ossau-iraty		Béarn-Basque country		R, T, I	F, A, I	AOC-AOP	6 months
Oustet		Ariège		R	F		6 months
Saint-lizier		Ariège		R	F, C		6 months
Tardets		Pyrenees		R	C		6 months
Tomme de brebis corse		Corsica		R	F, C		3 months
Tomme de brebis de Camargue		Camargue		R	F		1 year
Tomme des Grands Causses		Rouergue		R	F		8 months
Tommette du Pays Basque		Basque country		PP	C, I		1 month
Tourmalet		Béarn		R	C		2 months
Canestrato pugliese		Apuglia		R, P	C	AOC-AOP	1 year
Formaggio di fossa		Emilia-Romagna-Marche		R, P	C		3 months
Formaggio di Grotta Sulfurea		Emilia-Romagna		R	C		6 months
Pecorine lucano		Basilicata		R	C		3 months
Pecorino di Filiano		Basilicata		R	C		3 months
Pecorino di Moliterno	Canestrato di Moliterno	Basilicata		R	C		3 months
Pecorino di Pienza		Tuscany		R	C		6 months
Pecorino 'foja de noce'	Pecorino di Montefeltro, Caciotta di Montefeltro	Marche		R	C		2 months
Pecorino romano		Lazio-Sardinia-Tuscany		R, PP	C	AOC-AOP	9 months
Pecorino sardo	Fiore sardo – Pecorino fiore sardo	Sardinia		R	C	AOC-AOP	6 months
Pecorino siciliano	Canestrato siciliano	Sicily		R, P	F, C	AOC-AOP	6 months
Pecorino toscano	Pecorino toscanello	Tuscany		R, P	F, C, I	AOC-AOP	6 months
Piacintinu		Sicily		R	C		2 months
Acorn		Cardiganshire		R	C		6 months
Cwmtawe pecorine		Swansea		R	F		6 months
Evora				R	F, C	AOC-AOP	4 months

Idiazabal
Spain (Basque provinces and Navarre)
Ewe's milk

Idiazabal originated in the high Pyrenees, where the ewes
of the Lacha and Caranzana breeds ranged freely over the
mountains in summer. In September, when the weather
turned and the first cold spells arrived, the shepherds
came back down to the valleys with their cargo of
cheeses, slightly smoked after their prolonged stay
in mountain cabins heated by log fires. There is still
a smoked version of *Idiazabal*, made by farmers and
small cheesemakers; producers on an industrial scale
aren't aware of this variety. This characteristic product,
which often carries Basque emblems printed on its rind,
is made in a fairly stocky, cylindrical form. The cheese
is starred with a scattering of small holes; its texture
is quite dry but softens after ripening for six months.
In many ways it resembles the ewe's milk Tommes
from the French slopes but, on both sides of the frontier,
local loyalties have permitted each to retain its truly
individual character.

Family
Manchego
Country
Spain
Area of origin
Basque Country
and Navarre
Animal species
Ewe
Milk
Raw
Product
Farmhouse or
cottage industry
Optimum ripening
6 months

Laruns
France (Pyrenees)
Ewe's milk

Family
Manchego

Country
France

Area of origin
Pyrenees

Animal species
Ewe

Milk
Raw

Product
Cottage industry

Optimum ripening
6 months

Laruns – from the name of a town in the Ossau valley, in the Béarn region – is one of the main ewe's milk cheeses produced in the Pyrenees. In the past it was made largely on high mountain pastures from the end of spring to the beginning of autumn, in huts with the local name of *cajulas*. Hardly any was produced in winter. Nowadays, cheese dairies in the valley collect the milk from several sheep farms and keep up production all the year round. This cheese is a good introduction to the more ambitious products that are made exclusively in the mountain pastures in summer. Laruns, which weighs on average about 5 kilos (11 pounds), has a quite supple curd, with hardly any holes, protected by a thick rind – product of regular washing and drying. It can easily spend six months ripening in the cellar. The shepherds engrave their names on the rinds of farmhouse Laruns, so that they can identify their own products when they collect them from the *affineur* they entrusted with ripening them... who is paid in cheeses!

Lavort
France (Auvergne)
Ewe's milk

Though it is shaped like a cannonball, this cheese could not be less warlike. First made in 1988, it was the fruit of the fertile imagination of former dairy technician, Patrick Beaumont, who settled in Auvergne at Puy Guillaume, near Thiers. He went to southern Spain in search of suitable moulds, and decided to keep Lacaune sheep – a very rare breed in Auvergne (their milk is notably used to make Roquefort). Lavort is a pressed-curd cheese, which develops a quite soft consistency after four months ripening. It should not be matured for longer, because the thickening of the rind then becomes unstoppable, reducing the curd to an insignificant amount. The rind of Lavort is similar to that of Tomme de Savoie, but there the comparison ends. The character of the raw ewe's milk is revealed here by the very sharp, almost sweet, flavour that lingers interminably. Helped by his success, Patrick Beaumont encouraged young stockbreeders to establish herds and provide him with milk. Starting from nothing, this original product has managed, in the space of a few years, to carve out a niche for itself and find an undoubtedly permanent place on the already well-filled cheeseboards of Auvergne.

Family
Manchego
Other name
Médiéval
Country
France
Area of origin
Auvergne
Animal species
Ewe
Milk
Raw
Product
Farmhouse
Optimum ripening
3 months

Ossau-Iraty
France (Midi-Pyrenees)
Ewe's milk

Family
Manchego
Country
France
Area of origin
Béarn, French Basque
Country
Animal species
Ewe
Milk
Raw, pasteurized,
partially pasteurized
Product
Farmhouse, cottage
industry or industrial
Optimum ripening
6 months

Sheep have grazed in the Pyrenean mountains since time immemorial. The shepherds go up and spend the summer with their animals, making cheeses *in situ*. Each valley has its own version of ewe's milk Tomme, all expressing their local *terroir* and methods. Traditionally, the Bernese cheeses are more supple, with a more marked flavour than the Basque cheeses, which are drier and of smaller size. Having only recently been granted an AOC, Ossau-Iraty would like to think itself the product that sums up this long tradition. Together with Jean Etcheleku and his son Peyo, cheesemakers at Hellette, in the Basque country, I devised a 'made to measure' one. This cheese, made with raw milk from Mannech ewes, is matured for at least nine months and coated with Espelette peppers. An absolute delight with a thousand aromas! Each Tomme weighs from 4 to 4.5 kilos (9 to 10 pounds) and requires not less than 25 to 30 litres (40 to 50 pints) of milk. Jean and Peyo, who collect the milk from more than ninety farmers, select the choicest for me. At one time ewe's milk cheeses had a tendency to turn piquant, which is why the Basques drank very powerfully structured wines, such as Irouléguy, with them, or ate them with black cherry jam – *itxassou* – so that the sweetness masked this defect. They are no longer piquant but these combinations are still valid.

Pecorino Sardo
Italy (Sardinia)
Ewe's milk

In Italy, the name *Pecorino* covers a prolific and very varied family of cheeses, most of which are used grated, sliced or cut into slivers to flavour and embellish not only pasta but many other dishes. While we use them fresh, they like them as hard as stone. Their origins are lost in the mists of time (they were already known to Pliny the Elder). The only thing they have in common is their name, which means 'cheese made from ewe's milk'. Almost every region produces its own version, the best-known being *Pecorino Romano* (made both in Latium and Sardinia), *Pecorino Toscano* (made in Tuscany) and this *Pecorino Sardo* (also called *Fiore Sardo*), which is one of the most frequently exported varieties.

It is made in the form of a cylinder with a nicely curved crust; it can weigh up to 4 kilos (9 pounds) and rarely less than 1.5 kilos (3 pounds).

Benefiting from an AOC, it is a seasonal cheese, made largely in the early part of the year. The mild, *dolce* version, ripened from twenty to sixty days, has a soft curd; the hard, brittle *maturo* must be matured for at least a year. Like a great many pressed ewe's milk cheeses, *Pecorino Sardo* releases slightly lemony aromas when young and can become piquant as it ages.

Family
Manchego
Other names
Fiore Sardo
Pecorino Fiore Sardo
Country
Italy
Area of origin
Sardinia
Animal species
Ewe
Milk
Raw
Product
Cottage industry
Optimum ripening
6 months

Tomme des Grands Causses

France (Midi-Pyrenees)
Ewe's milk

Family
Manchego
Country
France
Area of origin
Rouergue
Animal species
Ewe
Milk
Raw
Product
Farmhouse
Optimum ripening
8 months

The Causses, arid lands in the south of the Massif Central, are among the best areas for the Lacaune breed of sheep. At Séverac, Simone Seguin and her son Rémi raise two flocks totalling 700 ewes. One flock gives milk during the first part of the year which goes to the makers of Roquefort; the other – the autumn flock – numbers just 200 and gives milk until Christmas which is sent to be made into Perail. Since the beginning of the 1990s, Simone and Rémi have been using a small part of their milk to make cheeses on their own account. Thus we have the Bleu de Séverac and this full-flavoured Tomme des Grands Causses, made almost entirely in the month of August, when the dairies specializing in Roquefort are closed. Weighing five kilos (11 pounds), it uses 25 to 28 litres (42 to 48 pints) of milk. Its slow development (six to eight months on pine boards) means it is ready for the spring fairs. It can be recognized by its thick, reddish rind and its quite supple texture. Its fruity flavour is splendidly complemented by red grapes as an accompaniment to an aperitif. It also comes in a version weighing 800 grams (28 ounces) – the Tommette des Grands Causses, which needs only three months ripening and graces the end-of-year festivities. You can run it to earth it at its 'birthplace' every Thursday during the summer, when Simone and Rémi open the farm to visitors.

Lavort (page 107); this cannonball-shaped cheese needs only 4 months ripening. Left for longer than that its rind thickens, to the detriment of the curd.

The Emmental family
and related cheeses

Easily recognizable by the large holes in its curd, this
cheese originated in Switzerland before being imitated
all over the world. Often produced by large, industrialized
cheese dairies, it is generally used in grated form.

Milk: R = raw, PP = partially pasteurized, P = pasteurized. Product: F = farmhouse, C = cottage industry, I = industrial.

Cheese	Other names	Country/Area of origin	Animal	Milk	Product	Label	Ripening
Alpsberg				P	I		6 months
Emmental bavarois	Allgäuer Emmentaler	Bavaria		P	I	AOC-AOP	4 months
Emmental autrichien				P	I		4 months
Murbodner				P	I		4 months
Tiroler alpkäse				R, P	I	AOC-AOP	6 months
Colombier des Aillons		Bauges		R, P	F, C		2 months
Emmental de Savoie		Northern Savoy – Savoy		R	I		6 months
Emmental français		Savoy – Northern Savoy		R, PP, P	C, I		6 months
Emmental grand cru		Franche-Comté – Savoy		R	I		6 months
Leerdamer		South		P	I		1 month
Maasdamer	Maasdam			P	I		1 month
Jarlsberg				P	I		6 months
Grevéost	Grevé			P	I		1 year
Emmental		Emme valley		R	C		1 year

The Gruyère family
and related cheeses

Originally from the Fribourg area, these cheeses, which sometimes contain small holes, were intended to be ripened for long periods; the curd is pressed to extract the maximum moisture. Their aromas develop very slowly but very intensely.

Milk: R = raw, PP = partially pasteurized, P = pasteurized. Product: F = farmhouse, C = cottage industry, I = industrial.

Cheese	Other names	Country/Area of origin	Animal	Milk	Product	Label	Ripening
Allgäuer bergkäse	Alpkäse	Bavaria	cow	R, P	C, I	AOC-AOP	1 year
Heidi gruyère		Tasmania	cow	P	C		18 months
Bergkäse				R	C		1 year
Beaufort		Beaufortin – Tarentaise – Maurienne	cow	R	F, C	AOC-AOP	12 months
Brouère, Le		North-east	cow	P	I		2 months
Comté	Gruyère de comté	Jura Mountains	cow	R	C	AOC-AOP	18 months
Graviera		Epirus, Crete	cow	P	I		6 months
Favorel			cow	P	I		6 months
Gabriel		Cork	cow	R	C		9 months
Asiago		North-east	cow	R	C	AOC-AOP	18 months
Asiago d'Allevo	Asiago d'Allievo	North-east	cow	R	C		18 months
Asiago grasso di monte		North-east	cow	R	C		18 months
Asiago pressato	Pressato	North-east	cow	R, P	I		1 month
Bergkäse		Alps	cow	R, P	C		6 months
Latteria		Friuli, Trentino, Veneto, Lombardy	cow	R, P	C		1 year
Montasio		Veneto-Friuli	cow	R, P	C, I	AOC-AOP	1 year
Monte veronese		Veneto	cow	R	C	AOC-AOP	2 years
Puzzone di moena		Trentino	cow	R	C		1 year
Silter		Lombardy	cow	R	C		1 year
Ubriaco		Veneto	cow	R, P	C		6 months
Vezzena		Trentino	cow	R, P	C		2 years
Étivaz, L'		Vaud canton	cow	R	F	AOC-AOP	18 months
Fribourg		French Switzerland	cow	R	C		18 months
Gruyère		French Switzerland	cow	R	C	AOC-AOP	18 months
Rebibes			cow	R	C		3 years
Spalen	Spalenkäse	Central Switzerland	cow	R	C		6 months
Tête-de-moine	Bellelay	Bernese Jura	cow	R	C	AOC-AOP	6 months

Asiago
Italy (North-east)
Cow's milk

Family
Gruyère
Country
Italy
Area of origin
North-east
Animal species
Cow
Milk
Raw
Product
Cottage industry
Optimum ripening
18 months

From the high plateau of Asiago, this cheese was originally made with ewe's milk but this has been completely ousted by cow's milk. It comes in two radically different forms, depending on how it is matured. The most usual one, *Assiago Pressato*, is eaten when it is about one month old. It is often made from pasteurized milk and its flavour is quite mild. Very much a universal cheese, it offends no one. The *Asiago d'Allevo* is cheese of a very different calibre. It hides beneath a thick brown rind and can be eaten *mezzano* (six months old) or *vecchio* (one year old). At that stage it is, *par excellence*, a candidate for the cheeseboard. Then, with the passing months, it dries out and shrinks. An *Asiago d'Allevo stravecchio* (two years old) has a dry, almost crumbly texture; when grated it is marvellous for cooking, adding intense flavour to many dishes – risotto in particular. Simply by using different ripening methods, a single cheese gives two very different results

Beaufort
France (Rhône-Alpes)
Cow's milk

Of all the Gruyère cheeses, Beaufort is undoubtedly the most sensual on the palate. Unlike most of that family of cheeses it is made with full-cream milk. This is also the reason why, as it ages, its full-bodied flavour tends to develop more quickly. Another characteristic, shared with Tomme d'Abondance and Italian Fontina, is its inward-curving rim – an infallible way of distinguishing it from so many other Gruyère cheeses. Made in the Tarentaise, Maurienne and Beaufortin regions, it is quite an imposing cheese, 10 centimetres (4 inches) thick with a diameter that can reach 75 centimetres (30 inches). It requires no less than 400 litres (700 pints) of milk to make one cheese, which explains why Beaufort is a 'community' cheese, made with milk from several herds, grazing together in a group. The cowman going to the high pastures in the summer will take herds belong to several farmers with him – as many as 200 animals. The acme of quality from the appellation, Beaufort Chalet d'Alpage, is made twice a day, exclusively on the high pastures at an altitude of more than 1,500 metres (5,000 feet). Produced only by a dozen chalets, it is truly exceptional!

Family
Gruyère
Country
France
Area of origin
Beaufortin, Tarentaise, Maurienne
Animal species
Cow
Milk
Raw
Product
Farmhouse or cottage industry
Optimum ripening
12 months

Comté

France (Franche-Comté)
Cow's milk

Family
Gruyère
Other name
Gruyère de Comté
Country
France
Area of origin
Jura Mountains
Animal species
Cow
Milk
Raw
Product
Cottage industry
Optimum ripening
18 months

Comté is a typical mountain cheese that takes up huge quantities of milk. One large round cheese – 65 centimetres (2 feet) in diameter and weighing 50 kilos (110 pounds) – is made with between 500 and 600 litres (100 and 125 gallons) of milk. The zone covered by the AOC is restricted to the Jura Massif and each cheese-maker is only allowed to collect milk within a 25 kilometre (15 mile) radius. In France and in Switzerland, these cheese dairies are known in the profession as *fruitières* (literally, places where the milk is 'fructified'). There are more than two hundred of them, producing Comté according to very strict specifications as to quality. The cheese is made from raw milk, from cows fed on fresh grass or hay (no silage, since this may contain ferments that cause the cheeses to split) and additives and colourings are forbidden. The spectacular traditional method involving the use of a cloth has almost disappeared; cheesemakers used a big linen cloth to collect the grains of curd – in suspension in the whey – from the vat, plunging their arms deep into the steaming liquid. Like good wine, Comté's most precious ally is time. The minimum ripening period is four months but it needs at least 18 months to develop all its aromas. Impatience can do it irreparable harm.

Gruyère
Swiss Romande
Cow's milk

Apart from being a cheese, Gruyère is also the name of
a charming little mediaeval-looking town in the Fribourg
Canton in Swiss Romande. The name, which is not
protected, is used all over the world and the average
consumer uses it erroneously for any large, firm cheese,
from Beaufort to Emmenthal, via Comté. Traditionally,
therefore, Gruyère is Swiss. Evidence of it goes back
to the beginning of the twelfth century. It is made in the
shape of a great wheel, up to sixty or more centimetres
(two feet or more) in diameter. Beneath the rind, the
cheese is quite firm and can have a scattering of pea-size
holes ('eyes', in cheesemakers' jargon). Any *lainures* – small
horizontal cracks – are an indication that it is over-ripened.
Half of the entire production comes from the Fribourg
Canton, about one third being made in the summer on
high pastures. Swiss *affineurs* offer a Gruyère known as
'reserve', which come from a selection of cheeses matured
for at least eight months. Gruyère is generally at its best
between 12 and 18 months.

Family
Gruyère
Country
Switzerland
Area of origin
Swiss Romande
Animal species
Cow
Milk
Raw
Product
Cottage industry
Optimum ripening
18 months

Tête-de-Moine

Switzerland

Cow's milk

Only 10 to 15 centimetres (4 to 6 inches) in diameter, Tête-de-Moine (monk's head) is a semi-hard lightweight, a stocky little cheese from the country that makes imposing wheels of Gruyère; but this doesn't mean it lacks character. It owes its name to Napoleon who re-named it after an advance during his invasion of Switzerland. With its top removed, it reminded him of a monk's tonsure. The fairly small production zone (the districts of Franches-Montagnes, Moutier and Courtelay), covers an area at the relatively modest altitude of 1,000 to 1,200 metres (3,200 to 4,000 feet). A dozen or so dairies produce this supple-textured cheese with a taste like that of Gruyère, which owes much of its success to a clever little gadget called a *girolle*. This allows you to scrape the cheese and form it into rosettes, curls and shavings, useful for serving with an aperitif or as garnish for a dish. This invention dates from the beginning of the 1980s and has literally caused an explosion in sales. Tête-de-Moine is usually matured for three or four months, but it can easily survive a good two months more.

Family

Gruyère

Other name

Bellelay

Country

Switzerland

Area of origin

Bernese Jura

Animal species

Cow

Milk

Raw

Product

Cottage industry

Optimum ripening

6 months

The Parmesan family
and related cheeses

A great Italian speciality, these cheeses, with their extra-hard, dry and granular texture and their strong flavour, are primarily used as a seasoning for any number of dishes. Some of them are matured for as long as four years.

Milk: R = raw, PP = partially pasteurized, P = pasteurized. Product: F = farmhouse, C = cottage industry, I = industrial.

Cheese	Other names	Country/Area of origin	Animal	Milk	Product	Label	Ripening
Parmesello				P	I		6 months
Creusois		Limousin Marche		R, P	F		6 months
Mizen		Cork		R	C		1 year
Bagos		Lombardy		R	C		1 year
Bitto		Lombardy		R	C	AOC-AOP	1 year
Grana		North		R, P	C, I		18 months
Grana padano		Northern Italy – Po river valley		R	C, I	AOC-AOP	2 years
Grana trentino		Trentino		R	C		2 years
Parmigiano reggiano		Lombardy – Emilia-Romagna		R	C, I	AOC-AOP	3 years
Västerbottenost	Västerbotten	Bothnia		P	I		1 year
Saanen	Hobelkäse	Fribourg		R	C		2 years
Sbrinz		Central Switzerland		R	C		18 months
Schabzieger	Sapsago (Suisse romande) – Kraüterkäse (Suisse alémanique)	Eastern Switzerland		R, P	C		2 months

Sbrinz
Central Switzerland
Cow's milk

Family
Parmesan
Country
Switzerland
Area of origin
Central Switzerland
Animal species
Cow
Milk
Raw
Product
Cottage industry
Optimum ripening
18 months

Sbrinz (the z is pronounced like an s) is thought to be one of the oldest Swiss cheeses; it is known to have existed in the fifteenth century. It is very like the Reggiano Parmesan made on the Italian side of the Alps, sharing with it the same need for a long ripening period (as much as four years) and the same crumbly, very dry texture which consigns it to use in the kitchen. One cheese weighs on average about 40 kilos (90 pounds). The cheese is ripened in a fairly warm cellar. Its intense, concentrated, very aromatic flavour goes marvellously with any dish; sprinkled on in grated form, it brings out all the flavour. Jacques-Alain Dufaux, retailer and *affineur* at Morges, recommends serving it with an aperitif in the form of small cubes or shavings, and letting it melt on the tongue accompanied by a dry white wine made from the Chasselas grape, which is grown in the same region. For the last three years its producers have been redefining the *terroir* where it originated, centred at the foot of the summit of mount Rigi, in the Lucerne region of central Switzerland. It is the third most exported Swiss cheese, after Gruyère and Emmenthal.

The date of production is marked on the rind of *parmiggiani* cheeses, as well as the dairy number and the 'parmiggiano reggiano' stamp, once quality approved. Then they are plunged into a brine bath.

The Raclette family
and related cheeses

Produced in the past in less isolated areas than those producing Gruyère, these wheel-shaped cheeses have a supple texture and a milder flavour. The curd is heated to a lesser degree and these cheeses can be eaten much younger, principally as raclette.

Milk: R = raw, PP = partially pasteurized, P = pasteurized. Product: F = farmhouse, C = cottage industry, I = industrial.

Cheese	Other names	Country/Area of origin	Animal	Milk	Product	Label	Ripening
Cave cheese		🇩🇰	🐄	P	I		4 months
Danbo		🇩🇰	🐄	P	I		6 months
Elbo		🇩🇰	🐄	P	I		6 months
Fynbo		🇩🇰	🐄	P	I		6 months
Samsø		🇩🇰	🐄	P	I		6 months
Tybo		🇩🇰	🐄	P	I		6 months
Abondance	Tomme d'Abondance	Northern Savoy – Chablais	🐄	R, P	F, C, I	AOC-AOP	6 months
Morbier	Faux septmoncel	Franche-Comté	🐄	R, P	F, C, I	AOC-AOP	4 months
Raclette		Alps	🐄	R, P	F, C, I		2 months
Almkäse		Bolzano province	🐄	R	C		1 year
Fontal		Aosta valley	🐄	P	I		3 months
Fontella		Aosta valley	🐄	P	I		3 months
Fontina		Aosta valley	🐄	R	F, C	AOC-AOP	6 months
Fontinella		Aosta valley	🐄	P	I		3 months
Formai de mut dell'alta val brembana		Lombardy	🐄	R	C		6 months
Mezzapasta		Piedmont	🐄	R, P	C		1 year
Ossalano bettelmatt		Piedmont, Ossola valley	🐄	R	C		1 year
Herrgårdsost			🐄	P	F, C, I		6 months
Anniviers		🇨🇭	🐄	R	C		6 months
Appenzeller		Appenzell canton	🐄	R	C		3–6 months
Bagnes		🇨🇭	🐄	R	C		6 months
Onches		🇨🇭	🐄	R	C		6 months
Forclaz		🇨🇭	🐄	R	C		6 months
Gomser		🇨🇭	🐄	R	C		6 months

Cheese	Other names	Country/Area of origin	Animal	Milk	Product	Label	Ripening
Orsières		🇨🇭	🐄	R	C		6 months
Raclette (fromage à)		🇨🇭	🐄	P	C, I		6 months
Rasskaas		🇨🇭 Appenzell canton	🐄	R	C		6 months
Saint-niklauss		🇨🇭 Valais	🐄	R	C		6 months
Schweizer mutschli		🇨🇭	🐄	R	C		3 months
Tilsit	Royalp	🇨🇭 Saint-Gall-Thurgau	🐄	R, P	C		6 months
Vacherin fribourgeois		🇨🇭 Valais	🐄	R	C		6 months
Valais	Raclette du Valais (fromage à)	🇨🇭 Valais	🐄	R	C		6 months

Abondance

France (Rhône-Alps)
Cow's milk

Family
Raclette
Other name
Tomme d'Abondance
Country
France
Area of origin
Northern Savoy, Chablais
Animal species
Cow
Milk
Raw
Product
Farmhouse, cottage
industry or industrial
Optimum ripening
6 months

It needs 60 to 70 litres (110 to 120 pints) of milk to make a wheel of Abondance, easily recognized by its inward-curving sides, which are reminiscent of a Beaufort. Abondance comes from Chablais, in the northern Alps, below Lake Leman. It is made in much the same way as the Gruyères, with the essential difference that the curd is slightly heated, giving a softer texture. This means that Abondance doesn't take as long to ripen as Beaufort – six weeks is enough for it to be at its best. It has a characteristic supple, even melting, texture. The farmhouse cheeses have a square patch of blue casein on the rind; those made in the dairy have an oval one.

My friend Daniel Boujon, retailer at Thonon-les-Bains and great connoisseur of cheeses from Savoie, likes the very typical little bitter touch found in Abondance and reserves his praise for cheeses made by small producers in the high pastures. He often says, 'Dairy-produced cheeses are like a beautifully written page with no crossings-out – but totally without character. The farmhouse product develops an aroma that even the best of the dairy products never achieves. Admittedly it occasionally has flaws, perhaps lacks the perfect little round holes required by the AOC, but these defects often give it richness and are the sign of a great cheese.' I couldn't agree more.

Appenzeller
Eastern Switzerland
Cow's milk

Appenzeller has a secret; it is matured with the aid of a mixture of herbs (the composition of which is jealously guarded) that give it a very distinctive flavour. The Appenzeller commercial cheese office distributes this aromatic mixture to about 100 cheesemakers and a dozen or so participating *affineurs*. Some of them personalize it by adding pepper, for example. It is impossible to find out any details. Appenzeller is regularly rubbed with this brine, which helps a rind (called *morgée*) to develop. It is already mature after three months but it will not show its full potential until after six months and will reach complete maturity at the end of ten months.

It is made in the north-east of Switzerland, an area of moderately high mountains. Its texture is similar to that of Raclette, its flavour close to that of the Gruyères. The labels are colour-coded: a silver background for the basic cheese, ripened for a minimum of three months; gold for the *surchoix* (prime quality), at least four months, and black for the *extra-vieux* (extra-old), which is at least six months old.

Family
Raclette
Country
Switzerland
Area of origin
Appenzell Canton
Animal species
Cow
Milk
Raw
Product
Cottage industry
Optimum ripening
3–6 months

Morbier

France (Franche-Comté)
Cow's milk

Would this cheese be as successful without its characteristic black stripe? In the old days it smelled deliciously of ash; when the milk was cooked in a cauldron hung over a wood fire, cheesemakers used to rub their hands around its blackened sides and coat the curd with soot to protect it. When wood fires were replaced by gas, they collected soot from the chimney and sifted it over the curd. Nowadays organic charcoal (sold in all chemist's shops) is used instead of soot. The dark stripe, ranging from black to blue-grey, is now merely a decorative reminder of the cheese's origins and imparts no particular flavour. Made throughout the Jura massif, generally in the *Comté fruitières*, Morbier begins to acquire real character after three to four months of ripening. Recently covered by an AOC, it will never have the strength and richness of Comté, which is made from the same milk, but it is notable for the very agreeable creaminess of its texture and its delicate, fruity aromas.

Family
Raclette
Other name
Faux Septmoncel
Country
France
Area of origin
Franche-Comté
Animal species
Cow
Milk
Raw or pasteurized
Product
Farmhouse, cottage industry or industrial
Optimum ripening
4 months

Saint-Niklauss
Switzerland (Valais)
Cow's milk

Originally from the Rhône valley, raclette dates back to the Middle Ages. It was the people of Valais who first thought of heating a cheese in front of the fire and scraping off the top layer as it melted. Nowadays we have small pans heated by electric elements to facilitate making it. Undoubtedly the best raclette is that made with Bagnes – known as raclette cheese in Switzerland. Sadly, it is a rare product – practically a limited edition – made on the summer mountain pastures, and hardly ever exported. The ones from the Anniviers, Conches and Ornières regions are very well known. As for Saint-Niklauss, it is a very well-reputed commercial brand; personally I extend the ripening period to almost five months. The curd needs to retain a certain firmness. Raclette has been widely promoted in France in the winter sports resorts. Traditionally it is eaten with baked potatoes and small pickled onions and gherkins. The dried meats from the Graubünden canton, or raw ham also go well with it. Like all up-market cheeses, products from the Valais have given rise to many imitations made with pasteurized milk. It is hoped that a projected AOC will put an end to this.

Family
Raclette
Country
Switzerland
Area of origin
Valais
Animal species
Cow
Milk
Raw
Product
Cottage industry
Optimum ripening
6 months

Vacherin Fribourgeois

Switzerland (Valais)
Cow's milk

Originally from the Fribourg canton in Swiss Romande, Vacherin Fribourgeois owes its reputation to its combination of very soft texture and strong flavour. Always made from raw milk, it comes in the form of a wheel, 30 to 40 centimetres (12 to 16 inches) in diameter. In the past there were two kinds of Vacherin: one used in fondue, a hard-pressed one made in winter and a handmade Vacherin – a softer product of autumn. This is no longer the case and the most prestigious cheeses are now made in mountain chalets. They are sold under the name of Vacherin Fribourgeois Alpage. According to how long they have been ripened, they may also be marked 'Select' (12 weeks), or 'Extra' (17 weeks). One can use Vacherin Fribourgeois equally well on the cheeseboard (the Swiss say they 'eat it with their fingers') or made into a fondue, where it will greatly enhance the flavour. Vacherin Fribourgeois is traditionally used in the so-called 'half-and-half' recipe for fondue, together with Gruyère de Fribourg. Those matured for a long period can be used to make 'shavings' for nibbling with an aperitif.

Family
Raclette
Country
Switzerland
Area of origin
Valais
Animal species
Cow
Milk
Raw
Product
Cottage industry
Optimum ripening
6 months

Making Morbier (page 126) at
La Chapelle-du-Bois.

The Stilton Family
and related cheeses

Cheeses veined with blue mould now form a prolific family since cheesemakers (undoubtedly those from the Auvergne) found out how the blue could be produced systematically by piercing the cheese with fine needles.

Milk: R = raw, PP = partially pasteurized, P = pasteurized. Product: F = farmhouse, C = cottage industry, I = industrial.

Cheese	Other names	Country/Area of origin	Animal	Milk	Product	Label	Ripening
Bergader				P	I		2 months
Blue bayou		Bavaria		P	I		3 months
Edelpilzkäse				P	I		3 months
Montsalvat				P	I		2 months
Paladin				P	I		2 months
Blue Cheshire		Cheshire		R, P	I		4 months
Blue vinny	Blue veiny – Dorset blue	Dorset		P	I		2 months
Blue Wensleydale		Yorkshire		P	I		2 months
Buxton blue		Derbyshire		P	I	AOC-AOP	3 months
Devon blue		Devon		R	C		3 months
Dovedale blue				P	I	AOC-AOP	3 months
Oxford blue		Oxfordshire		P	C		3 months
Shropshire blue		Shropshire		P	I		3 months
Stilton	Blue Stilton – White Stilton	Leicestershire		P	C, I	ACO-AOP	6 months
Bla Castello	Castello blue			P	I		3 months
Danablu	Danish blue cheese – Danblue – Marmora			P	I	IGP	3 months
Jutland blue				P	I		2 months
Layered blue				P	I		2 months
Mellow blue				P	I		2 months
American blue				P	I		2 months
Blue cheese				P	I		3 months
Maytag blue		Iowa		R	C		6 months
Aura				P	I		2 months

Cheese	Other names	Country/Area of origin	Animal	Milk	Product	Label	Ripening
Bleu d'Auvergne		Auvergne	cow	R, PP, P	I	AOC-AOP	6 months
Bleu de Bonneval		Vallée de Bonneval – Haute-Maurienne	cow	R	C		2 months
Bleu de Brissac		Auvergne	cow	R	C		6 months
Bleu de Cayres		Auvergne	cow	R	C		6 months
Bleu de Costaros		Auvergne	cow	R	F		3 months
Bleu de Gex	Bleu du Haut-Jura – Bleu de Septmoncel	Franche-Comté	cow	R	C, I	AOC-AOP	2 months
Bleu de la Planèze		Auvergne	cow	R	C		6 months
Bleu de Langeac		Auvergne	cow	R	C		2 months
Bleu de Laqueuille		Auvergne	cow	P	F, C, I		3 months
Bleu de Loudès		Auvergne	cow	R	C		2 months
Bleu de Pontgibaud		Auvergne	cow	R	C		6 months
Bleu de Thiézac		Auvergne	cow	R	C		6 months
Bleu de Tulle		Auvergne	cow	R	C		6 months
Bleu des Causses		Aveyron-Lot-Lozère-Gard-Hérault	cow	R, PP, P	C, I	AOC-AOP	6 months
Bleu du col Bayard	Petit bayard	Dauphiné-Provence	goat	R, PP	C		1 month
Bleu du Quercy		Quercy	cow	P	I		3 months
Carré d'Aurillac		Auvergne	cow	P	F		1 month
Fourme d'Ambert		Auvergne	cow	R, PP, P	F, C, I	AOC-AOP	4 months
Fourme de la Pierre-sur-Haute		Auvergne	cow	R	C, I		4 months
Fourme de Montbrison		Auvergne	cow	R, PP, P	F, C, I	AOC-AOP	4 months
Fourme du Forez		Forez	cow	R, PP, P	C		4 months
Velay	Fromage aux artisons	Auvergne	cow	R	F		3 months
Cashel blue	Cashel Irish blue	Tipperary	cow	P	F		4 months
Strachitùnd	Erborinato di artavaggio	Lombardy-Val Taleggio	cow	R, P	C, I		3 months
Oryzae			cow	P	I		1 month
Adelost	Ædelost		cow	P	I		2 months

Bleu de Gex

France (Franche-Comté)
Cow's milk

Family
Stilton

Other names
Bleu du Haut-Jura
Bleu de Septmoncel

Country
France

Area of origin
Franche-Comté

Animal species
Cow

Milk
Raw

Product
Cottage industry
or industrial

Optimum ripening
2 months

This fairly dry, blue-speckled cheese was first made by monks but it was the medical profession that extended its popularity beyond the Jura, where it is made. Starting in the twelfth century the monks of the Sainte-Claude Abbey undertook the clearance of the high ground, opening the way, first to sheep and goat farming and then to cattle. Two centuries later a 'grey cheese' made its appearance – the forerunner of the Bleu de Gex. The establishment of coal mines in the Stephanoise region opened up new markets for it. The doctors who looked after the miners recommended this cheese to them because it contained penicillium – or so I am told by Isabelle Seignemartin, highly regarded cheese-*affineur* specializing in Bleu de Gex. The Saint-Étienne region, where they prefer chalky textures, is still a major market for it. My customers like them ripened for about two-and-a-half to three months, when they develop a softer texture and more pronounced blue colour. In the Jura they are used to make raclette and soufflées. Always made with raw milk, the tiny hint of bitterness is an integral part of its flavour. Isabelle's grandfather used to collect the milk from 65 farms. Today it is made by only three cheese dairies, but the future of Bleu de Gex gives no cause for alarm.

Bleu des Causses

France (Midi-Pyrenees)
Cow's milk

Bleu des Causses is a cow's milk version of Roquefort. My impassioned colleague Jean Puig, from Montpellier, tells me that not all that long ago some farmers still mixed ewe's milk with the cow's milk. Bleu des Causses has undoubtedly been in existence for several centuries. Made in an area of poor and stony soil, it was ripened in the caves that abound on these rough, chalky plateaux. It has retained its well-structured nature and its straightforward, lively flavour. A few cheese dairies – there are no longer any farmhouse producers – continue to produce it. It needs to ripen in a damp, cool cellar for at least three months. The curd is pricked at the start of production to help oxygenate it and allow the blue to develop. Jean Puig assures me, from his own experience, that Bleu des Causses is rounder on the palate, finer, less rustic and less salty than the much better-known Bleu d'Auvergne. The old tradition of drinking a robust wine of the region with it no longer holds good; Bleu des Causses has been promoted and now goes well with sweet wines, the sugar content softening its temperament. Jean Puig recommends further accompanying it with dried figs, cut into fine strips, and a piece of rye bread. A feast fit for a king!

Family
Stilton
Country
France
Area of origin
Aveyron, Lot, Lozère, Gard, Hérault
Animal species
Cow
Milk
Raw, pasteurized or partially pasteurized
Product
Cottage industry or industrial
Optimum ripening
6 months

Bleu du Col Bayard

France (Provence-Côte d'Azur)
Goat's milk

The cheese dairy at Col Bayard, in the Hautes-Alpes, is installed in the quite steep, high Champsaur Valley. There is not a great deal of pasture there but its quality is excellent. The farms have always produced blue cheese made with goat's milk – an unusual recipe. The dairy revitalized the tradition in 1978 with this cheese, which is like a firmer, rather smaller version of Bleu de Sassenage, or the Bleu de Queyras that is made in the next valley. It is made entirely with 'mountain milk', collected at an altitude of more than 1,000 metres (3,000 feet), and processed raw or partially pasteurized. It weighs about 200 grams (7 ounces) and has a distinctive character, combining the flavour of goat's milk cheese with the strength of blue cheese. Eminently suitable for the cheeseboard, it can also be used in sauces to accompany meat. If you wish, you can taste it in the dairy's own restaurant. There, in addition to a cheese museum, you will find other products made by the dairy, such as Chaudun – an original soft-pressed cheese made from 25 per cent goat's milk, 25 per cent ewe's milk and 50 per cent cow's milk – or the Tommette de Brebis, ripened with Alpine yarrow. The Tommette is macerated for 40 days in alcohol with a few sprigs of yarrow and 40 lumps of sugar. And that is (almost) all there is to know about it!

Family
Stilton
Other name
Petit Bayard
Country
France
Area of origin
Dauphiné, Provence
Animal species
Goat
Milk
Raw or partially pasteurized
Product
Cottage industry
Optimum ripening
1 month

Fourme d'Ambert

France (Auvergne)
Cow's milk

Married for a time, Fourme d'Ambert and Fourme de Montbrison have decided to go their separate ways: both covered by the same AOC, they wish to resume their 'maiden names' to avoid being mistaken for each other, as happened with Munster and Géromé, or with Valençay and Levroux. While they both come from the slopes of the Mont du Forez, Montbrison faces east and Ambert west. The latter is recognized by its dry, grey rind, with occasional little red patches. The former, ripened on pine racks, is an attractive, orange-ish colour. The curd of the Fourme d'Ambert is 'wilder', more veined with blue than that of Montbrison. This amicable divorce, which has already resulted in them holding separate fairs, is not just a Clochemerle affair; it comes within the framework of the renaissance movement, and demonstrates how culturally attached the local people are to their product. In 1996, after a twenty-year absence, a farmhouse Fourme d'Ambert – made with raw milk – has re-emerged. I make no secret of my support for these cheese producers, who have an acute sense of *terroir*.

Family
Stilton
Country
France
Area of origin
Auvergne
Animal species
Cow
Milk
Raw, pasteurized or partially pasteurized
Product
Farmhouse, cottage industry or industrial
Optimum ripening
4 months

The Gorgonzola Family
and related cheeses

These blue-veined cheeses have a much creamier texture than those of the Stilton type. Their flavour is, on the whole, less pronounced, no doubt because their production is now very industrialized.

Milk: R = raw, PP = partially pasteurized, P = pasteurized. Product: F = farmhouse, C = cottage industry, I = industrial.

Cheese	Other names	Country/Area of origin	Animal	Milk	Product	Label	Ripening
Bayerhofer blue		Bavaria	cow	P	I		2 months
Bleu de Bavière		Bavaria	cow	P	I		1 month
Cambozola			cow	P	I		1 month
Montagnolo			cow	P	I		2 months
Exmoor blue		Somerset	cow, deer, sheep	R	F	IGP	2 months
Lymeswold			cow	P	I		2 months
Gippsland blue		Victoria	cow	P	C		3 months
Milawa blue		Victoria	cow	P	C		3 months
Mycella			cow	P	I		2 months
Dunsyre blue		Lanarkshire	cow	R	C		3 months
Bleu de Bresse	Bresse bleu		cow	P	I		2 months
Bleu du Vercors-Sassenage		Vercors	cow	R, P	F, I	AOC-AOP	3 months
Montbriac		Auvergne	cow	P	C		15 days
Saingorlon			cow	P	I		2 months
Saint-agur		Forez	cow	P	I		1 month
Bavaria blu			cow	P	I		1 month
Dolcelatte		Lombardy	cow	P	I		3 months
Dolcelatte torta		Lombardy	cow	P	I		1 month
Gorgonzola		Piedmont-Lombardy	cow	P	C, I	AOC-AOP	4 months

Bleu du Vercors-Sassenage
France (Vercors)
Cow's milk

Bleu de Vercors-Sassenage is the most 'Italian' of the French blue cheeses, with its milder and slightly less creamy texture that bears some resemblance to certain types of Gorgonzola. Quite different from its close relatives of the Massif Central, it is all delicacy, balance, almost discretion. Not much given to extremes, its mould is a fairly pale blue and its soft, melt-in-the-mouth texture tends to be supple and elastic. It is excellent for cooking – delicious as raclette or fondue. This is a fairly atypical cheese, made by mixing the evening's milk, which is pasteurized, with the raw product of the next morning's milking – a technique that harks back to ancient times when the Vercors peasants had to boil the evening's milk to keep it from turning sour. Pasteurization before its time! The cheese originated on the Vercors plateau (formerly known as 'Monts de Sassenage'), a true natural fort amid extensive farming land. All of the farmhouse producers gave up in the 1950s and for half a century only one cheese dairy continued to make this blue cheese. When Vercors was declared a nature reserve, the influx of tourists created a demand that resulted in a dozen farmers taking up the trade.

Family
Gorgonzola
Country
France
Area of origin
Vercors
Animal species
Cow
Milk
Raw or pasteurized
Product
Farmhouse or industrial
Optimum ripening
3 months

The Cabrales family
and related cheeses

The family of blue goat's milk cheeses is a very small one, largely centred on Spain. The blue appears in the form of fairly irregular marbling; the flavour is incomparable.

Milk: R = raw, PP = partially pasteurized, P = pasteurized. Product: F = farmhouse, C = cottage industry, I = industrial.

Cheese	Other names	Country/Area of origin	Animal	Milk	Product	Label	Ripening
Beenleigh Blue		Devon		R	C		8 months
Harbourne blue		Devon		R	C		2 months
Chèvre-Noit		Eastern cantons		P	C		3 months
Cabrales	Cabraliego	Asturia		R, PP	F, C	AOC-AOP	6 months
Gamonedo		Gamoneu		R	F, C		6 months
Picón		Cantabrian Mountains		R	C		3 months
Picos de Europa		Cantabrian Mountains		R, P	F, C		3 months
Champignon de luxe				P	I		1 month
Blue Rathgore		North		P	I		6 months

The Roquefort family
and related cheeses

Ewe's milk gives these most glorious of the blue cheeses something extra by way of strength and spirit that makes them easily distinguishable from cheeses made from cow's milk. What a pity that they are sometimes used to make sauces!

Milk: R = raw, PP = partially pasteurized, P = pasteurized. Product: F = farmhouse, C = cottage industry, I = industrial.

Cheese	Other names	Country/Area of origin	Animal	Milk	Product	Label	Ripening
Yorkshire blue		🏴 Yorkshire	🐑	P	F		2 months
Meredith blue		🇦🇺 Victoria	🐑	P	C		2 months
Bleu de la Moutonnière		🇨🇦 Bois-Francs	🐑	P	C		4 months
Lanark blue		🏴 Lanarkshire	🐑	R	F, C		3 months
Bleu de Brach	Tomme de Brach	🇫🇷 Limousin	🐑	R	C		3 months
Bleu de Corse		🇫🇷 Corsica	🐑	R	F		2 months
Bleu de Séverac		🇫🇷 Aveyron	🐑	R	F		3 months
Roquefort		🇫🇷 Rouergue	🐑	R	F, C, I	AOC-AOP	6 months

Bleu de Séverac

France (Midi-Pyrenees)
Ewe's milk

Family
Roquefort
Country
France
Area of origin
Aveyron
Animal species
Ewe
Milk
Raw
Product
Farmhouse
Optimum ripening
3 months

Traditionally the cheese dairies that produce Roquefort only work during the first half of the year, when the yield from the ewes is abundant. They close their doors on 27th July and stop collecting the milk. For some time now, while waiting for the ewes to cease lactating in mid-September the farmers of the region have made either Pérail, or this blue cheese. Bleu de Séverac, its name taken from that of the village 30 kilometres (18 miles) from Millau, is thus a kind of Roquefort, though it cannot be called that because it is not ripened at Roquefort-sur-Soulzon. Simone Séguin launched it more than 20 years ago, following in the footsteps of her mother and her mother-in-law, who made a ewe's milk blue-veined cheese at the end of the season. There is no question of competing with Roquefort on its own terms; Bleu de Séverac is smaller, with a more supple curd, yellower in colour and less strong on the palate. Simone, helped by her son Rémi, ripens it for as much as two months or more, in an old vaulted wine cellar, but I like to extend that by up to two further months. Perhaps we are witnessing at the birth of a future farmhouse Roquefort. But for that Simone and Rémi would have to acquire a disused cellar in the village of Roquefort. Watch this space...

Roquefort cheeses in the process of ripening.

The Termignon family
and related cheeses

This small family is made to a very unusual recipe, which involves heating the curd. The flavour is quite acidic, the blue appears spontaneously, in an irregular manner, in the form of veining and marbling.

Milk: R = raw, PP = partially pasteurized, P = pasteurized. Product: F = farmhouse, C = cottage industry, I = industrial.

Cheese	Other names	Country/Area of origin	Animal	Milk	Product	Label	Ripening
Bleu de Termignon		Haute-Maurienne		R	F		6 months
Castelmagno		Piedmont		R	F, C	AOC-AOP	6 months
Murianengo		Piedmont		R	F		6 months

Denis Provent, *affineur* at Chambéry, flexing his muscles cutting a Bleu de Termignon, a seasonal cheese produced in fairly limited quantities.

Bleu de Termignon

France (Rhône-Alpes)

Cow's milk

Family

Termignon

Country

France

Area of origin

Haute-Maurienne

Animal species

Cow

Milk

Raw

Product

Farmhouse

Optimum ripening

6 months

Bleu de Termignon is unlike any other cheese. Produced in the high mountain pastures at the end of the Vanoise valley, it is made from 're-cooked' curd, in which the blue appears spontaneously, in the form of veining and marbling. High in fat, its texture is crumbly and granular. The very unusual method by which it is made gives the flavour a little hint of cooked whey, and sometimes it resembles Salers. Difficult and unpredictable, this cheese presents a unique profile. The five cheese dairies that still produce it are largely run by women, several of them young ones whose presence gives reassurance that this very sought-after cheese will be with us for a long time to come. Denis Provent told me that it took him five years to master the technique of ripening it to perfection. He pricks the cheeses to help foster the blue veining. The cows graze on pastures at an altitude of 2,000 metres (6,500 feet) and their milk is particularly rich. There were already cows there, it seems, in the time of the Dukes of Savoie. Bleu de Termignon is highly prized on the other side of the frontier; the Italians from the Aosta valley, who used to bring their cows to pasture in France, became absolutely besotted by it, and still continue to eat it regularly.

The Brillat-Savarin family
and related cheeses

The double-cream and triple-cream cheeses are, as the saying goes, the 'foie gras' of cheeses. These products certainly don't skimp on the addition of cream to make their generous, satiny textures a delight on the palate.

Milk: R = raw, PP = partially pasteurized, P = pasteurized. Product: F = farmhouse, C = cottage industry, I = industrial.

Cheese	Other names	Country/Area of origin	Animal	Milk	Product	Label	Ripening
Double cream cheese		🇬🇧	cow	P	C, I		1 month
Finn		🇬🇧 Hereford-Worcester	cow	R	F		1 month
Prince Jean		🇫🇷	cow	P	C		1 month
Bonde	Bondard – Bondon	🇫🇷 Normandy	cow	R, P	F, C		1 month
Bouille		🇫🇷 Normandy	cow	P	C		2 months
Boursault		🇫🇷 Brie	cow	P	I		1 month
Brillat-savarin		🇫🇷 Normandy-Burgundy	cow	R,PP, P	C, I		1 month
Châteaubriand	Magnum	🇫🇷 Normandy	cow	P	C, I		2 months
Clovis		🇫🇷 Burgundy	cow	P	C		1 month
Croupet		🇫🇷 Normandy-Burgundy	cow	P	I		3 weeks
Délice de Pommard		🇫🇷 Burgundy	cow	P	C		2 weeks
Délice de Saint-Cyr		🇫🇷 Brie-Burgundy	cow	PP, P	I		1 month
Excelsior		🇫🇷 Bray region	cow	P	C, I		2 months
Explorateur		🇫🇷 Île-de-France	cow	R	C, I		3 weeks
Fin-de-siècle		🇫🇷 Normandy – Bray region	cow	P	C		3 weeks
Fromage de Monsieur	Monsieur fromage	🇫🇷 Normandy – Calvados	cow	P	I		3 weeks
Grand Vatel		🇫🇷 Burgundy	cow	P	C		1 month
Gratte-paille		🇫🇷 Brie	cow	R	C		1 month
Lucullus		🇫🇷 Brie	cow	P	I		3 weeks
Pierre-Robert		🇫🇷 Brie	cow	R	C		1 month
Royal briard		🇫🇷 Île-de-France	cow	P	C		6 weeks
Saint-gildas-des-bois		🇫🇷 Brittany	cow	P	C		1 month
Suprême		🇫🇷 Normandy	cow	P	C, I		2 months

Délice de Pommard

France (Burgundy)

Cow's milk

This is a really original cheese, in shape as well as in flavour. Délice de Pommard was created around 1996, by a Burgundy cheese-merchant, Alain Hess, *affineur* and retailer at Beaune. He started with an ordinary fresh triple-cream cheese, which he flavoured with mustard or, more precisely, with mustard-seed bran. Since this has neither the same strength, nor even quite the same taste as mustard, the great majority of consumers were unable to guess the source of its strange and seductive aroma. The cheese is dipped into the mustard bran, then kneaded and hand-moulded with a cloth, which gives it the shape of a fresh fig. It was an immediate success, and a number of restaurants have found a place for it on their cheeseboards. Imitations were not slow to appear. Délice de Pommard is best eaten when still fresh, at the end of a meal. Alain Hess, who tried garlic and many different herbs before coming up with the winning idea, tells me he is busy working on a new revolutionary product.

Family

Brillat-Savarin

Country

France

Area of origin

Burgundy

Animal species

Cow

Milk

Pasteurized

Product

Cottage industry

Optimum ripening

2 weeks

Explorateur

France (Île de France)
Cow's milk

Explorateur – so named in honour of the space shuttle Explorer – was first made in the 1950s, in a cheese dairy in the Seine-et-Marne region. It is a commercial brand name. It is one in a long line of cheeses enriched with fresh cream, starting in 1890 with the Excelsior, popularized by the Brillat-Savarin (re-launched in 1930 by Henri Androuët), then given a boost in the post-war years. With the rigours of rationing over, these cheeses, with their satiny texture and their good aroma of cream, were a symbol of abundance and regained prosperity. There have been any number of imitations – mostly in Normandy and Île de France – including this 'Explorer', which only needs to be ripened for two or three weeks. Is it as rich in fat as one would suppose from reading the 75 per cent on the label? This figure is misleading, because it refers to the percentage of the total milk solids in the cheese made up by fat – in other words, 75 per cent of the weight of the cheese without its water content. Since a product like Explorateur contains almost 80 per cent water, especially when fresh, this puts a different perspective on the fat-content figure.

Family
Brillat-Savarin
Country
France
Area of origin
Île-de-France
Animal species
Cow
Milk
Raw
Product
Cottage industry
or industrial
Optimum ripening
3 weeks

Gratte-Paille

France (Île-de-France)

Cow's milk

This cheese was created in the 1960s by the Rouzaire Company of Seine-et-Marne. It is a triple-cream cheese enriched with fresh cream, which gives it a particularly generous and delicate texture and, when young, a very distinct flavour of cream and butter. It is a variant of Brillat-Savarin – a similar cheese created between the two World Wars by Henri Androuët. Very knowledgeable about this type of cheese, my colleague, Sylvie Boubrit – a cheese retailer in Paris – is one of the people for whom Gratte-Paille holds no secrets. She never tires of saying that this is a cheese that deserves rediscovering. In her opinion it has more flavour than a Brillat-Savarin or a Pierre-Robert, on condition that it is ripened for up to ten weeks. But not more, for the cheese becomes too strong after that.

In the cellar, one has to guard against allowing it to 'turn', which would leave it with a predominant salty or bitter flavour. Though it is available in all seasons, it is in spring and during end-of-year festivities that this generous cheese finds its most devoted following. Sylvie cordially recommends a white wine from Quercy to drink with it. Can you guess where the name *gratte-paille* (scratch-straw) comes from? It is that of a bush that grows beside lanes and catches on the straw piled on passing carts.

Family
Brillat-Savarin

Country
France

Area of origin
Brie

Animal species
Cow

Milk
Raw

Product
Cottage industry

Optimum ripening
1 month

Royal Briard
France (Île de France)
Cow's milk

All the cheese *affineurs* in the Paris region offer their own version of Brillat-Savarin, triple-cream cheese invented at the start of the last century. This is not because they are attempting to usurp it for their own purposes, but because great skill is required to ripen this fairly delicate type of product. It is not unknown for bitter, soapy flavours to form beneath the rind if it is not properly handled. Practically speaking, everything hangs on the first days after the cheese is made. In particular, the *affineur* must pay close attention to the onset of mould and the way in which the cheese gives up its water-content in the *haloirs* (drying rooms). Gerard Gratiot, *affineur* in Hauts-de-Seine and specialist in soft-pressed and bloomy-rind cheeses from Île de France, offers this Royal Briard, made in Seine-et-Marne and ripened in his cellars at Asnières. He works on it for four to six weeks. The cheese gradually loses weight in the *haloir*, sometimes going from 600 grams (20 ounces) down to 450 grams (14 ounces). Its rich, creamy paste makes it truly a 'special occasion' cheese. Indeed, most of it is sold at Christmas and New Year or Easter.

Family
Brillat-Savarin
Country
France
Area of origin
Île-de-France
Animal species
Cow
Milk
Pasteurized
Product
Cottage industry
Optimum ripening
6 weeks

The Chabichou family
and related cheeses

The more or less compact tower or plug shape is quite common in goat's milk cheeses. Made with lactic curd, they generally become dry when ripened.

Milk: R = raw, PP = partially pasteurized, P = pasteurized. Product: F = farmhouse, C = cottage industry, I = industrial.

Cheese	Other names	Country/Area of origin	Animal	Milk	Product	Label	Ripening
Capricorn Goat		🏴 Somerset	🐐	P	I		1 month
Chabis Sussex goat cheese		🏴 Sussex	🐐	R	F		1 month
Autun		🇫🇷 Burgundy	🐄 🐐	R	F		15 days
Bonde de Gâtine		🇫🇷 Deux-Sèvres	🐐	R, P	F		1 month
Bouca		🇫🇷 Centre	🐐	R	F		15 days
Bressan		🇫🇷 Bresse	🐐	R	F		2 weeks
Cabardès		🇫🇷 Aude	🐐	R	F		1 month
Chabichou du Poitou		🇫🇷 Haut-Poitou	🐐	R, PP, P	F, C, I	AOC-AOP	1 month
Charolais	Charolles	🇫🇷 Burgundy – Charolais	🐐	R	F, C		1 month
Civray		🇫🇷 Poitou-Charentes	🐐	R	F		2 weeks
Clacbitou		🇫🇷 Burgundy	🐐	R	F, C		1 month
Cornilly		🇫🇷 Berry	🐐	R	C		3 weeks
Dornecy		🇫🇷 Nivernais	🐐	R	F		1 month
Fourme de chèvre de l'Ardèche		🇫🇷 Rhône-Alps	🐐	R	F		2 months
Gien		🇫🇷 Orleans region	🐄 🐐	R	F, C		1 month
Mâconnais	Chevreton de Mâcon	🇫🇷 Burgundy –	🐐	R	F, C		2 weeks
	Cabrion de Mâcon	Maçon region					
Montoire		🇫🇷 Orleans region	🐐	R	F		3 weeks
Montrachet		🇫🇷 Burgundy	🐐	R, P	F		3 weeks
Troo		🇫🇷 Orleans region	🐐	R	F		3 weeks
Villageois		🇫🇷 Charentes	🐐	R	F, C		3 weeks
Villiers-sur-Loir		🇫🇷 Orleans region	🐐	R	F		3 weeks
Mine-Gabhar		🇮🇪 Wexford	🐐	R	F		1 month

Bonde de Gâtine

France (Poitou-Charentes)
Goat's milk

This cheese was created to order at the end of the 1970s.
A dairywoman in Saint-Germain-en-Laye was looking
for a cheese along the lines of a Selle-sur-Cher,
but twice the height. She talked to Louis-Marie
Barreau, a small goat breeder at Verruyes in the
Deux-Sèvres region, who embarked on a series
of trials and came up with Bonde de Gâtine.
This has been a registered trademark since 1978.
The dairywoman had real flair – the Gâtine region
has always been a favoured area for stock breeding.
Let Louis-Marie tell you himself: 'As its name indicates,
this region is blessed, with its woods and hedges, valleys
and chestnut forests – very like Normandy. The land, which
is clay, is left permanently to pasture.' With a dimension
of 7 centimetres (2.7 inches) in both height and diameter,
Bonde is a stocky little cheese. It is made with less than
2 litres (3 pints) of raw milk which is coagulated
immediately after every milking and hand-ladled into
moulds. A real farmhouse cheese. I heartily agree with
Louis-Marie (who now processes the milk from two
neighbouring farms), when he says that Bonde is
nondescript if eaten fresh. He ripens it for 45 days, after
which time its paste has tightened up and developed the
sweet flavour typical of goat's milk cheeses.

Family
Chabichou
Country
France
Area of origin
Deux-Sèvres
Animal species
Goat
Milk
Raw or pasteurized
Product
Farmhouse
Optimum ripening
1 month

Chabichou du Poitou

France (Poitou-Charentes)
Goat's milk

Family
Chabichou
Country
France
Area of origin
Haut-Poitou
Animal species
Goat
Milk
Raw, Partially pasteurized
or pasteurized
Product
Farmhouse, cottage
industry or industrial
Optimum ripening
1 month

Nicknamed 'Chabis', its full title is 'Chabichou du Poitou
AOC'. Six centimetres (2.3 inches) high, this little goat's
milk cheese's truncated cone shape – the diameter
decreasing slightly from base to summit – is easily
recognized. It is sold in a range of qualities, from the
authentic farmhouse products made from raw milk, to
the more commonplace pasteurized industrial cheese for
which Poitou has become a centre. You can tell the farmhouse
ones – those made by the Georgelet Company, for example –
by their impeccably smooth texture, resulting from very careful
moulding by hand. They are really excellent after three to four
weeks ripening. A small historical note: 'Chabichou' could
be a corruption of the Arab word *chebi*, meaning 'little goat'.
Every French schoolchild learns that Charles Martel halted
the Arab advance at Poitiers in 732.
It was more probably a brief incursion by a War Lord intent
on pillaging the countryside, but what does it matter as long
as the Saracens left behind their recipe for a cheese made from
goat's milk? In fact, goats were depicted in local engravings
long before the time of Charles Martel, so the mystery of the
origins of Chabichou has still to be solved.

Charolais

France (Burgundy)
Goat's milk

In all the Charolais mountain areas the goats are overshadowed by the prestigious local cattle, the Charolais. The announcement that an AOC was to be granted for Charolais, the local goat's milk cheese, gained the nanny goats a little bit more respect. And they can be proud of their classy, tower-shaped cheese, which is notable for its dense and compact texture. Bernard Sivignon – a successor to the *Racotiers* of years gone by, who went from farm to farm collecting cheeses, chickens, eggs and rabbits – is one of the great architects of this development. He ripens (under the name of Clacbitou) the produce from fifty or so farmers, mostly women who have followed in their mothers' footsteps. It needs 2 to 2.5 litres (3.5 to 4.3 pints) of milk to make one cheese according to a method which demands patience and delicacy (slow coagulation, hand-ladling into moulds, draining over several days, etc.); that's the price that must be paid for a 'marble curd' – very smooth and homogeneous without being brittle. Well-ripened (up to four weeks), Charolais offers aromas of almonds and hazelnuts. The presence of a blue mould on the rind – as long as it is not too pronounced – gives it the taste of mushrooms and of the cellar.

Family
Chabichou
Other name
Charolles
Country
France
Area of origin
Burgundy, Charolais
Animal species
Goat
Milk
Raw
Product
Farmhouse or cottage industry
Optimum ripening
1 month

Mâconnais
France (Burgundy)
Goat's milk

Smaller than its neighbour Charolais, which is made in much the same way, Mâconnais only weighs between 50 and 70 grams (1.75 and 2.5 ounces), according to how long it has been ripened. Like Crottin de Chavignol, its small size is due to it having been originally made in the vineyards, where the vine growers' plots were often very small. Each of them kept a goat or two, which fed on the grass along the roadsides. The quantity of milk they gave was only enough to make small cheeses, which served to feed the workers. Today, more than 400 farmers produce this little cheese, and it can only be a question of time before it is given an AOC. Locally it is eaten fairly fresh, six days after it is taken out of the moulds. After two or three weeks it begins to develop a fine growth speckled with blue. Its curd is quite fine and very slightly acidic. In the Mâcon vineyards it is often eaten as a snack at ten in the morning, with a little glass of white wine – a Mâcon-Village, for example, or a Pouilly-Fuissé.

Family
Chabichou
Other names
Chevreton de Mâcon
Cabrion de Mâcon
Country
France
Area of origin
Burgundy,
Mâcon region
Animal species
Goat
Milk
Raw
Product
Farmhouse or
cottage industry
Optimum ripening
2 weeks

The Brique du Forez family
and related cheeses

Generally made from curd coagulated with rennet, unlike the previous category these cheeses become creamy as they ripen; the more so because of their relatively slender shape. Their flavour is quite mild.

Milk: R = raw, PP = partially pasteurized, P = pasteurized. Product: F = farmhouse, C = cottage industry, I = industrial.

Cheese	Other names	Country/Area of origin	Animal	Milk	Product	Label	Ripening
Brique ardéchoise		Ardèche		R	F		1 month
Brique du bas Quercy		Rouergue		R	F		1 month
Brique du Forez		Monts du Forez		R, P	F, C		1 month
Brique du Livradois	Cabrion	Livradois		P	F		1 month
Briquette d'Allanche		Cantal		R	F		3 weeks
Briquette de la Dombes		Dombes		R	F, C		2 weeks
Chêne		Quercy		R	F		2 weeks
Lingot ardéchois		Ardèche		R	F		1 month
Lingot du Berry		Berry		P	C		1 month
Rieumoise		Pyrenees		R	F		1 month
Saint-Nicolas-de-la-Dalmerie		Haut-Languedoc		R	F		1 month

Briquette d'Allanche

France (Auvergne)
Goat's milk

Family
Brique du Forez
Country
France
Area of origin
Cantal
Animal species
Goat
Milk
Raw
Product
Farmhouse
Optimum ripening
3 weeks

This goat's milk Briquette is unusual for the Cantal mountains, where the cows – pride of the region – leave little room for nanny goats. It is made, from raw milk, by a stockbreeder who keeps sixty goats in the Allanche region (Cézallier), in the north of the department. The farm is perched on a plateau up at 1,000 metres (3,200 feet) set aside essentially for summer pasturing. The cows are taken up there in May, staying until autumn. The goats, however, stay up there all the year round. They are dry during December and January – so no Briquette during that time! The ripening of this delicate cheese, which tends to become acidic if kept for long periods, is fairly short – from two to three weeks. The skin becomes very slightly knobbly, while the curd remains smooth, becoming more or less creamy according to season. A real treat! My brother Alain, who finds Briquette sells like hot cakes in his shop at Saint-Flour, stocks the fairly young ones that are to his local customers' taste. For those cheeses that are more mature and full-flavoured he has a different use; they are cut into small slices, placed on a slice of toast together with a slice of the local ham, grilled, and eaten with a salad. Whenever I visit Cantal to see my family, I never fail to avail myself of this simple piece of pure pleasure!

The Sainte-Maure family
and related cheeses

This family undoubtedly owes its popularity
it its practical shape, which is easy to cut.
Almost all are cheeses made from lactic curd,
which dries as it matures.

Milk: R = raw, PP = partially pasteurized, P = pasteurized. Product: F = farmhouse, C = cottage industry, I = industrial.

Cheese	Other names	Country/Area of origin	Animal	Milk	Product	Label	Ripening
Golden Cross		🏴 Sussex	🐐	R	C		1 month
Rosary Plain		🇬🇧 Wiltshire	🐐	R	F		2 weeks
Bouchon lyonnais		🇫🇷 Lyons region	🐐	R	F		1 month
Bûchette d'Anjou		🇫🇷 Anjou	🐐	R	C		15 days
Bûchette de Banon		🇫🇷 Provence	🐐	R	F		1 week
Chouzé		🇫🇷 Berry	🐐	P	I		3 weeks
Graçay		🇫🇷 Berry	🐐	R	C		1 month
Île d'Yeu		🇫🇷 Île d'Yeu	🐐	R	F		1 month
Joug		🇫🇷 Berry	🐐	R	F, C		1 month
Ligueil		🇫🇷 Berry	🐐	P	I		3 weeks
Loches		🇫🇷 Berry	🐐	P	I		3 weeks
Saint-loup		🇫🇷 Berry	🐐	P	I		3 weeks
Sainte-maure		🇫🇷	🐐	R, P	F, C, I		15 days
Sainte-maure-de-Touraine		🇫🇷 Touraine	🐐	R	F, C	AOC-AOP	1 month
Tournon-saint-pierre		🇫🇷 Touraine	🐐	R	F		1 month
Vazerac		🇫🇷 Quercy	🐐	R	F		3 weeks

Sainte-Maure-de-Touraine

France (Central)
Cow's milk

Far from the flamboyance of the Mediterranean and the opulence of Normandy, Touraine delights in muted measures and a refined ambience, as typified by the sun rising on the morning mists over the Loire. The 'Garden of France' has produced a cheese that fits this image of finesse and refinement: Sainte-Maure-de-Touraine.

Made from raw milk, it is identified by its balanced flavour and its very fine grain. About 30 centimetres (12 inches) long, it is usually pierced from end to end by a straw which in former days allowed farmers to stick broken cheeses back together again or reinforce them. Woe betide anyone who cuts the first piece from the narrow end; according to the old saying, this is 'cutting the goat's udder'. Almost a hundred farmers produce this delicate cheese, imitated throughout France under the name of 'Sainte-Maure'. The flavour is influenced by the seasons; in summer it gives off aromas of dried hay, changing to nutty flavours in the autumn. It is white when young and bluish after ripening for three weeks to a month, or it can be *cendré*, according to an old technique, which improves its keeping qualities. A sparkling Vouvray is always a happy accompaniment.

Family
Sainte-Maure
Country
France
Area of origin
Touraine
Animal species
Goat
Milk
Raw
Product
Farmhouse or
cottage industry
Optimum ripening
1 month

The Bougon family
and related cheeses

This is a Camembert-type goat's milk cheese, with a white bloomy rind. In the professional jargon of the cheese-maker, the modern, pasteurized-milk version of this is called *chèvre boîte* – (boxed goat's milk cheese).

Milk: R = raw, PP = partially pasteurized, P = pasteurized. Product: F = farmhouse, C = cottage industry, I = industrial.

Cheese	Other names	Country/Area of origin	Animal	Milk	Product	Label	Ripening
Bougon		▮▮ Poitou-Charentes	🐐	R	I		2 weeks
Cathare		▮▮ Laurageais	🐐	R	F		1 month
Chabris		▮▮ Touraine – Berry	🐐	R	F		1 month
Mothe-saint-héray		▮▮	🐐	P	I		1 month
Saint-cyr		▮▮ Poitou-Charentes	🐐	P	I		3 weeks

The Carré du Tarne family
and related cheeses

Square cheeses seem to be losing popularity
with consumers, for some mysterious and
incomprehensible reason. Here are a few
survivors that are not afraid of angles.

Milk: R = raw, PP = partially pasteurized, P = pasteurized. Product: F = farmhouse, C = cottage industry, I = industrial.

Cheese	Other names	Country/Area of origin	Animal	Milk	Product	Label	Ripening
Cabra		Corsica		R	C		6 weeks
Calenzana		Northern Corsica		R	F		3 months
Carré de Chavignol		Centre		R	C		1 month
Chèvrefeuille	Chèvre à la feuille	Deux-Sèvres		R	C		1 month
Couhé-vérac		Poitou		R	F, C		1 month
Curac	Pavé du Quercy	Quercy		R	F, C		15 days
Fleur du maquis	Brindamour – Brin d'amour	Corsica		R	F, C		3 months
Fleury du col des Marousses		Pyrenees		R	F		6 weeks
Lauzeral		Quercy		R	F		1 month
Mascaré		Provence		R	C		1 month
Mouflon		Southern Corsica – Calgese		R	F		3 months
Pavé ardéchois		Ardèche		R	F		1 month
Pavé blésois		Blois		R	F		1 month
Pavé de Gâtine		Poitou-Charentes		R	F		1 month
Pavé de la Ginestarie	Carré du Tarn – Pavé du Tarn	Albigeois		R	F		1 month
Pavé des Dombes		Dombes		R	F, C		2 weeks
Saint-maixent		Poitou		R	F		1 month
Sublime du Verdon		Verdon		R	F		1 month
Tarnisa		Quercy		R	C		15 days

Fleur du Maquis
France (Corsica)
Ewe's milk

Fleur du Maquis – flower of the Corsican scrubland – is the most famous of the Corsican cheeses, also known under the commercial name of Brin d'Amour. I particularly like the recipe concocted by Claudine Vigier, retailer-*affineur* at Carpentras. She perfected it after experimenting for four years. She starts with fresh Tommes, which are delivered from Corsica. She ties each cheese in a little cloth, knotting it to give it the desired shape, and leaves it overnight to drain. The next day she removes the cloth and sets the curd on a plank in a draught of air. She turns it regularly for several days, then she moistens the surface and rolls it in a skilfully chosen mixture of herbs: oregano, savory, rosemary, a touch of pimento, juniper and a few grains of pepper. The cheeses are then covered with film and left in the cellar for three days, after which the film is removed and they are put in a wooden chest with more herbs for another ten days to a fortnight. At the end of that time, beneath the herbs and spices is a creamy paste with the good, honeyed taste of ewe's milk. Claudine only makes Fleur du Maquis from November to the end of June – the ewes' lactation period.

Family
Carré du Tarn
Other names
Brindamour, Brin d'amour
Country
France
Area of origin
Corsica
Animal species
Ewe or goat
Milk
Raw
Product
Farmhouse or cottage industry
Optimum ripening
3 months

Mascaré

France (Provence-Côte d'Azur)
Goat's and ewe's milk

Family
Carré du Tarn
Country
France
Area of origin
Provence
Animal species
Ewe or goat
Milk
Raw
Product
Cottage industry
Optimum ripening
1 month

This square-shaped cheese is very popular in the Forcalquier region, where it is eaten creamy. It is original in that it is made with a mixture of raw milk from both goats and ewes in the true tradition of all cheeses from Provence where, because of the animals' different lactation cycles, the peasants used whichever milk was available. The modern mania for regulation and calibration had not yet taken hold.

Mascaré is well balanced on the palate, the ewe's milk softening its 'goaty' character. It is wrapped in a chestnut leaf and its top adorned by Provençal herbs. My colleague, Claudine Mayer, originally from Auvergne, is very taken with this cheese, which she ripens to great effect. She has just opened a shop equipped with magnificent, twelfth-century vaulted cellars at Saint-Rémy-de-Provence. The Mascaré cheeses are splendidly at ease there, like all the other Provençal specialities she is so fond of – fresh Tomme des Alpilles, in olive oil, Camarguais (a pressed-curd ewe's milk Tomme), Trident (fresh Tomme made with ewe's milk from the Arles region). She may invite you to taste her Mascaré with a white wine from the Baux valley. Quite simply, pure pleasure!

Pavé de Gâtine
France (Poitou-Charente)
Goat's milk

Pavé de Gâtine was created by thirty-year-old farmer, Sébastien Gé. His parents came to Deux-Sèvres in 1976, with no previous knowledge of cheese-making but more than willing to learn. Sébastien took over from them in 1995 and keeps a herd of about a hundred goats, the whole of whose milk yield he makes into cheese. The farm is 25 kilometres (15 miles) north of Niort, in an area which is very like Brittany, with standing stones, weighing several tons, resembling menhirs. Sébastien makes about two hundred cheeses a day, including this square-shaped Pavé de Gâtine, which is made from raw milk and ladled into the mould. It takes two litres (3.5 pints) of milk to make one Pavé. Because the cheese is not very thick, it must be ripened with great care. A slight white down of *Geotrichum* forms on the surface with a scattering of blue *penicillium*. When the cheese is well drained in the *hâloir* (drying room), Sébastien places it on a chestnut leaf to make it look attractive. He collects the leaves from the trees himself in the autumn and dries them by the fire, then stores them in a fairly dry place. His reward is the renown of this smooth, creamy Pavé, fêted year after year at the regional goat's milk cheese fair held at Niort at the beginning of May.

Family
Carré du Tarn
Country
France
Area of origin
Poitou-Charentes
Animal species
Goat
Milk
Raw
Product
Farmhouse
Optimum ripening
1 month

Pavé de la Ginestarie

France (Midi-Pyrenees)
Goat's milk

This thick Pavé (from 2.5 to 3 centimetres (0.9 to 1.2 inches) makes no attempt to hide its origins; the goat taste is very pronounced. It is made in the Tarn region by Dragan and Chantal Téotski, who also produce Coeur Téotski. Their 45 hectares (110 acres) are farmed organically. Apart from a short period in winter, the 150 goats roam outside almost all year round. Fond of hazelnuts and acorns, they like to graze in the areas bordering the woods and undergrowth. This diet inevitably ends up influencing the aromas of the cheese. Pavé de la Ginestarie (the name of the area) is ripened for three to four weeks. Day by day it shrinks, losing a good centimetre (third of an inch) of its original size. The curd is particularly fine-grained – the quality of the milk produced by the flock and the ladle moulding have played their part. This Pavé is particularly good with white wine. Dragan recommends a Gaillac.

Family
Carré du Tarn
Other names
Carré du Tarn,
Pavé du Tarn
Country
France
Area of origin
Albigeois
Animal species
Goat
Milk
Raw
Product
Farmhouse
Optimum ripening
1 month

The Chavignol family
and related cheeses

Crottins came into being in poor wine-growing areas where the milk that the agricultural workers obtained from their goats was insufficient to make larger cheeses. Stocky and rustic, these cheeses are often very close textured.

Milk: R = raw, PP = partially pasteurized, P = pasteurized. Product: F = farmhouse, C = cottage industry, I = industrial.

Cheese	Other names	Country/Area of origin	Animal	Milk	Product	Label	Ripening
Bilou du Jura		Jura		R	F		10 days
Bouchon de Sancerre		Sancerrois		R	F		1 month
Cabécou de Thiers		Auvergne		R	F		1 month
Caboin		Berry		R	F		3 weeks
Cathelain		Savoy		R	F		15 days
Châtaignier		Quercy		R	F		3 weeks
Chèvroton du Bourbonnais		Bourbonnais		R	F		3 weeks
Crézancy	Sancerre	Sancerrois		R	F		1 month
Crottin d'Ambert	Ambert	Auvergne		R	F		15 days
Crottin de Chavignol	Chavignol	Cher-Loiret-Nièvre		R	F, C, I	AOC-AOP	1 month
Lyonnais		Lyons region		R	F		3 weeks
Marchal		Lorraine		R	F		15 days
Quatre-vents		Dauphiné		R	F		3 weeks
Roncier		Vaucluse		R	F		2 weeks
Saint-amand-montrond		Sancerrois		R	F		1 month
Santranges		Sancerrois		R	F		1 month
Toucy		Burgundy		R	F, C		15 days
Vendômois		Vendômois		R	F		15 days

Cabécou de Thiers

France (Auvergne)
Goat's milk

Family
Chavignol
Country
France
Area of origin
Auvergne
Animal species
Goat
Milk
Raw
Product
Farmhouse
Optimum ripening
1 month

Trying out a different way of living, in near self-sufficiency, cocking a snook at society; these were very much the conditions in which this excellent little goat's milk cheese came into being, at an altitude of 650 metres (2,125 feet). Claire Guillemette, its creator, keeps a tiny herd of about 30 goats on the 35 hectares (86 acres) that surround her farm in the village of Thiers. The countryside, made up of moors, woods and a few hectares of meadows, is not very fertile, but her goats' needs are few and they seem happy to roam in the open air, gazing over the Puy de Sancy and the Puy de Dôme. For 25 years now Claire has been making this cheese, by a method similar to that used to make Cabécou. The milk is processed raw, with the addition of whey saved from the previous day, and the cheese is ladle moulded.

It is eaten fairly soft after ripening for 15 to 20 days. Its flavour is very balanced, almost sensual. Claire keeps chickens, makes bread, jams and sorbets, but for all that, she finds time to keep herself in the public eye (her cheese was first exhibited at the Saint-Maure-de-Touraine fair) and to apply European standards of manufacture.

The Dôme du Poitou family
and related cheeses

This quite recent family of cheeses is made in an original shape and seems set for a great future. In the case of goat's milk cheeses, often very similar in appearance, the shape can sometimes make all the difference.

Milk: R = raw, PP = partially pasteurized, P = pasteurized. Product: F = farmhouse, C = cottage industry, I = industrial.

Cheese	Other names	Country/Area of origin	Animal	Milk	Product	Label	Ripening
Dôme		Berry	🐐	R	F, C		3 weeks
Dôme du Poitou		Poitou	🐐	R	C		1 month
Petit fermier		Provence	🐐	R	F		3 weeks
Taupinière des Charentes		Poitou-Charentes	🐐	R	F		3 weeks
Truffe de Valensole		Haute-Provence	🐐	R	F		3 weeks

The Bouton de Culotte (trouser button) family
and related cheeses

These cheeses are, of course, intended to
accompany an aperitif. They can be eaten
either fresh or slightly ripened. Some of them
are flavoured with various herbs or spices.

Milk: R = raw, PP = partially pasteurized, P = pasteurized. Product: F = farmhouse, C = cottage industry, I = industrial.

Cheese	Other names	Country/Area of origin	Animal	Milk	Product	Label	Ripening
Grabetto		Victoria		P	C		1 month
Apérobic		Burgundy		R	F		10 days
Baratte de chèvre		Burgundy		R	F		10 days
Bouton d'oc		Midi-Pyrenees		R	F		10 days
Bouton de culotte		Burgundy		R	F, C		4 weeks
Caillou du Rhône		Maçônnais		R	F, C		15 days
Chevry		Saône-et-Loire		R	F, C		2 weeks
Gasconnades		Gers		R	F		1 week
Rigotton		Val-d'Oise		R	F		15 days

Bouton de Culotte (trouser button)
France (Burgundy)
Goat's milk

The largest goat farm in Europe also produces the smallest cheese: Bouton de Culotte weighs only about 15 grams (half an ounce) when ripened, and twice as much in the fresh state. For Thierry Chévenet, the project grew out of a whim; in 1966, when he was still a small child, he asked his farmer parents for a goat. Since then, in the space of 25 years, he has built up a herd of 1,700 goats in the Saône-et-Loire region.

His farm combines the most up-to-date, sophisticated equipment (his goats carry electronic implants so they can be traced) and traditional methods: no silage; no vaccination or treatment for parasites, no skimming, animals put out to pasture whenever possible. The very few Bouton de Culotte that are produced are only offered to famous names. One of the first customers was Paul Bocuse, followed by his colleague Georges Blanc. It is one of those rare cheeses that can drain without being turned, thanks to its truncated cone shape. This is not due to mere chance; in this wine-making region the women were in the vineyards all day and only returned in the evening, which meant they were not able to turn the cheeses during the day. Bouton de Culotte is eaten very fresh – for breakfast, for example – if not, then almost dry after maturing for three to four weeks.

Family
Bouton de Culotte
Country
France
Area of origin
Burgundy
Animal species
Goat
Milk
Raw
Product
Farmhouse or cottage industry
Optimum ripening
4 weeks

The Pélardon family
and related cheeses

A great many goat's milk cheeses are made in the form of a disc of varying diameter and thickness. They are found in every region, without exception. The shape is used for cheeses made from both lactic curd and those coagulated with rennet.

Milk: R = raw, PP = partially pasteurized, P = pasteurized. Product: F = farmhouse, C = cottage industry, I = industrial.

Cheese	Other names	Country/Area of origin	Animal	Milk	Product	Label	Ripening
Bosworth		Staffordshire	goat	R	F		1 month
Cerney village		Gloucestershire	goat	P	F		1 month
Capriole banon	Indiana	Indiana	goat	P	F		1 month
Alpicrème		Alpilles	goat	R	F		2 weeks
Anneau de Vic-Bilh		Pyrenees	goat	R	F		2 weeks
Arôme à la gêne de marc	Arôme de Lyon	Lyons region	cow goat	R	C		3 months
Arôme au vin blanc		Lyons region	cow goat	R	C		3 months
Banon	Banon à la feuille	Provence	goat	R	F, C		1 month
Banon poivre		Provence	cow goat sheep	R	F, C		1 month
Banon sarriette		Provence	cow goat sheep	R	F, C		1 month
Beaujolais pur chèvre		Beaujolais	goat	R	C		1 month
Bigoton		Orleans region	goat	R	F		15 days
Bruyère de Joursac		Auvergne	goat	R	F		1 month
Cabécou d'Entraygues			goat	R	F		3 weeks
Cabécou de Cahors		Lot	goat	R	F		3 weeks
Cabécou du Béarn			goat	R	F		3 weeks
Cabécou du Fel		Quercy	goat	R	F		3 weeks
Cabécou du Périgord		Aquitaine	goat	R	F, C		3 weeks
Cabri de Parthenay		Deux-Sèvres	goat	R	F		15 days
Cabri des Gors		Deux-Sèvres	goat	R	F		3 weeks
Capri lezéen		Poitou	goat	R	F		15 days
Capricorne de Jarjat		Ardèche-Vivarais	goat	R	F		1 month
Cendré de la Drôme		Drôme provençale	goat	R	F		15 days
Château vert		Mont Ventoux	goat	R	F		15 days
Chèvre à la sarriette		Provence	goat	R	F		3 weeks
Chèvre affiné au marc de bourgogne		Burgundy	goat	R	F		1 month
Chèvre de l'Ariège		Pyrenees	goat	R	F		15 days

Cheese	Other names	Country/Area of origin	Animal	Milk	Product	Label	Ripening
Chèvre de Provence		Provence		R	F		1 month
Chèvre des Alpilles		Provence		R	F		3 weeks
Chèvre du Larzac		Larzac		R	F		2 weeks
Chèvre du Morvan		Morvan		R	C		3 weeks
Chèvre du Ventoux		Provence		R	F		2 weeks
Chevriou		Saône-et-Loire		R	F, C		1 month
Cujassous de Cubjac		Périgord		R	F		3 weeks
Fromage corse (Manenti)		Southern Corsica		R	F		2 months
Fromage du Jas		Provence		R	F		3 weeks
Galet de Bigorre		Pyrenees		R	F		2 weeks
Galet solognot		Orleans region		R	F		2 weeks
Galette de La Chaise-Dieu		Auvergne		R	F		1 month
Gavotine		Provence		R	F		1 month
Gramat		Quercy		R	F		1 month
Groû du Bâne		Provence		R	F		3 weeks
Livernon du Quercy		Quercy		R	F, C		3 weeks
Lunaire		Quercy		R	F		2 weeks
Lusignan		Poitou		R	C		3 weeks
Mont d'or du Lyonnais	Mont d'or de Lyon	Lyons region		R	F, C		1 month
Mothais sur feuille		Poitou		R	F		3 weeks
Pélardon		Cévennes		R	F, C, I	AOC-AOP	3 weeks
Pélardon des Corbières		Corbières		R	C		1 month
Petit pastre camarguais		Provence		R	F		3 weeks
Petit quercy		Quercy		R	F		3 weeks
Petite meule		Quercy		R	F		1 month
Picadou				R	F, C		3 weeks
Picodon		Rhône valley		R, PP, P	F, C	AOC-AOP	3 weeks
Poivre d'âne	Pèbre d'aï	Provence		R	F, C, I		15 days
Pougne cendré		Gâtine		R	F		1 month
Provençal		Provence		R	F, C		1 month
Rocamadour	Cabécou de Rocamadour	Quercy		R	F, C	AOC-AOP	2 weeks
Rogeret de Lamastre		Vivarais		R	F, C		1 month
Rond'oc		Tarn		R	F		3 weeks
Rouelle du Tarn	Rouelle blanche	Tarn		R	F		1 month
Ruffec		Poitou		R	F		3 weeks
Saint-félicien		Vercors		R, P	F, C, I		3 weeks
Saint-félicien de Lamastre		Vivarais		R	F		3 weeks

Cheese	Other names	Country/Area of origin	Animal	Milk	Product	Label	Ripening
Saint-gelais		■ ■ Poitou	🐐	R	F		3 weeks
Saint-héblon		■ ■ Périgord	🐄 🐐	P	C		3 weeks
Saint-mayeul		■ ■ Haute-Provence-Plateau de Valensole	🐐	R	F		1 month
Saint-nicolas de l'Hérault		■ ■	🐐	R	F		3 weeks
Saint-pancrace		■ ■ Rhône-Alps	🐐	R	F		3 weeks
Saint-rémois		■ ■ Saint-Rémy-de-Provence	🐐	R	F		15 days
Séchon		■ ■ Dauphiné	🐐	R	F		4 weeks
Selles-sur-cher		■ ■ Berry	🐐	R	F, C	AOC-AOP	15 days
Tomme capra		■ ■ Rhône valley	🐐	R	F		1 month
Tomme de Banon		■ ■ Provence	🐄 🐐 🐑	R	F, C		3 weeks
Tomme de chèvre d'Arles		■ ■ Provence	🐐	R	F		3 weeks
Tomme de Provence à l'ancienne		■ ■ Camargue	🐐	R	F		3 weeks
Tomme de Saint-Marcellin		■ ■ Dauphiné	🐄 🐐	R,PP, P	F, C, I		2 weeks
Tomme des quatre reines de Forcalquier		■ ■ Haute-Provence	🐐	R	F		1 month
Tommette à l'huile d'olive		■ ■ Provence	🐐	R	F		15 days
Vieillevie		■ ■ Lot	🐐	R	F		2 weeks
Robiola della langhe		■ ■ Piedmont-Cuneo Province	🐄 🐐 🐑	R,PP, P	C		3 weeks
Scimudin		■ ■ Lombardy	🐄 🐐	R, P	C		1 month

The most picturesque of the cheeses that are wrapped in leaves is Banon, (page 174) made in the *garrigues* of the Alps in Haute-Provence. The leaves are collected every autumn, either from the trees, or from the ground as soon as they have fallen. A skilled employee can wrap a hundred cheeses per hour.

Banon

France (Provence-Côtes d'Azur)
Goat's milk

Family
Pélardon
Other name
Banon à la Feuille
Country
France
Area of origin
Provence
Animal species
Goat
Milk
Raw
Product
Farmhouse or
cottage industry
Optimum ripening
1 month

Enveloped in chestnut leaves and tied with raffia, this colourful little Provençal cheese only sheds its wrappings just before being eaten.

It is a soft-curd cheese – made according to a method of heating the milk to speed up coagulation that is common to the whole of the Mediterranean basin, where the climate quickly causes the milk to deteriorate. This type of cheese becomes creamy as it ripens, whereas cheeses made with lactic curd – a slower method of coagulation – have a greater tendency to dry out.

One of my favourite producers is Noël Autexier, from the dry hills of the Forcalquier region. He keeps about 60 goats amid the bushes and shrivelled white oaks and practises biodynamic farming, sticking as far as possible to the natural breeding cycle. He also makes Pélardons and Tommes, but for him Banon is far and away the most demanding, requiring leaves to be collected daily from the trees in autumn, dried, scalded, folded. Noël employs a specialist 'folder' who can wrap a hundred cheeses an hour. At this stage the cheeses are sprayed with eau-de-vie. I personally am not in favour of ripening them for too long, as Banon becomes very strong after a certain time.

Bruyère de Joursac

France (Auvergne)

Goat's milk

A German couple now resident in France created this attractive cheese. In 1987, Claudia and Wolfgang Reuss, who had long been attracted to the Auvergne mountains, decided to leave the highly industrialized Stuttgart region and 'live off Nature and with Nature, in an atmosphere of peace and calm'. They settled in a lost corner at an altitude of 1,100 metres (3,600 feet), in an old farmhouse facing Mount Journal and its slopes covered with pine, ash and beech trees. In the verdant valley below there are many natural meadows on which their seventy-two goats graze from the end of March to November. Two years after their arrival, they began producing this little round cheese, with a beige-coloured natural rind enclosing a very smooth curd which, with a little coaxing, will develop a creamy texture.

To begin with, the couple sent their newly made cheeses to an *affineur* to be ripened but now, having become more confident, they ripen them themselves for at least a month. The name of the cheese is taken from the name of the locality, La Brugère, so called after the heather that abounds there. The cheese, which requires about 2.5 litres (4.25 pints) of milk, is particularly exquisite in May and June. Very fragrant, it literally melts on the tongue.

Family

Pélardon

Country

France

Area of origin

Auvergne

Animal species

Goat

Milk

Raw

Product

Farmhouse

Optimum ripening

1 month

Gramat

France (Midi-Pyrenees)
Goat's milk

Big brother of Rocamadour, Gramat is the only child of Marthe Pégourié, a prominent figure in the department of the Lot. This energetic cheese merchant, established in the village of Gramat, has appointed herself the mouthpiece for the traditional local produce, and has made an important contribution to its increased popularity. For thirty years she has collected cheeses from the neighbouring Causses region and ripened them in her cellars. She considers the Cabécous from Rocamadour too niggardly for her customers' taste and dismisses them as mere 'medallions' or 'discs'; the eight centimetre (third of an inch) diameter Gramat is much more acceptable to her. The methods she uses, on the other hand, are exactly the same as those of Rocamadour. This cheese also has the advantage of keeping better. Like the little Cabécou, Gramat becomes blue at the end of ripening. Marthe is at pains to explain to her customers – especially to the many tourists who stop at her shop convinced they are visiting a national monument – that Gramat is at its best once it has turned blue. Whatever you do, don't complain that the rinds of her cheeses have gone mouldy!

Family
Pélardon
Country
France
Area of origin
Quercy
Animal species
Goat
Milk
Raw
Product
Farmhouse
Optimum ripening
1 month

Mothais sur Feuille

France (Poitou-Charentes)

Goat's milk

Mothais sur Feuille originated in the south of the formerly fairly impoverished Deux-Sèvres region. On farms, the goat was looked upon as the 'poor man's cow'. The many chestnut forests in the area gave the farmers the idea of wrapping their cheeses in leaves to preserve them for household use in the winter. Later, the Mothais cheeses were collected for sale in local markets. Today, five or six farmers and several cheese dairies promote this delightful cheese, and are beginning to feel the need for a label recognizing it. One of its most enthusiastic representatives is Maryse Micheaud, of the Georgelet Company who, since 1975, has been making Mothais with the milk from her 650 goats. The milk is used raw and the curd is ladle moulded. The leaf is placed under the cheese as soon as it comes out of the strainer and functions as a regulator, soaking up the moisture from the cheese while at the same time preventing it from draining too quickly. The leaves are taken from the trees before they fall, in the two weeks following the first frosts. Mothais, similar in size to a Camembert, is at its best when very creamy. It may become covered with a very delicate blue mould.

Family
Pélardon

Country
France

Area of origin
Poitou

Animal species
Goat

Milk
Raw

Product
Farmhouse

Optimum ripening
3 weeks

Picodon

France (Rhône-Alpes)
Goat's milk

Family
Pélardon
Country
France
Area of origin
Rhône Valley
Animal species
Goat
Milk
Raw, Partially pasteurized
or pasteurized
Product
Farmhouse or
cottage industry
Optimum ripening
3 weeks

Made in the Ardèche and the Drôme, but also in a small part of the Gard and Vaucluse, Picodon is at its best from March onwards. Its AOC is somewhat wide-ranging and fairly heterogeneous in terms of quality. Anyway, it is the only cheese to have circled the world in the space shuttle: the French astronaut Jean-Jaques Favier took fourteen Picodon cheeses with him aboard the Columbia in April, 1996. It is true that, at seven centimetres (2.7 inches) in diameter it doesn't take up much room (in the Languedoc dialect *picho* means 'small'). The one I prefer comes from the Peytot farm in the Ardèche Cévennes. Christian Moyersoen keeps some hundred and twenty goats, looked after by a shepherdess among the chestnut woods, heather and broom. The farm stands at an altitude of about 750 metres (2,500 feet) at the end of a forest track. Christian arrives at the local markets, where most of his cheeses are sold, with fifteen different kinds of cheeses in separate boxes: blue Picodons, brown ones, black, white, rather dull-looking cheeses ripened by the 'méthode Dieulefit' (ripening in a damp cellar), etc. There is a positive explosion of milk products from February to April, but the bulk of consumption is in summer, when the tourists arrive, and during the end-of-year festivities. Which is why he is obliged to look after his cheeses and, therefore, to be aware of how best to ripen them – which he does brilliantly.

Pougne Cendré
France (Poitou-Charentes)
Goat's milk

Pougne Cendré has been in existence for at
least twenty years. Though it looks like a
smaller version of Selle-sur-Cher it is, in fact,
modelled on a Cendré de Niort. A mature
Pougne Cendré weighs about 150 grams
(5 ounces). It is made only by young farmer
Sébastien Gé, using a fairly traditional method.
Each cheese requires 1.25 litres (2 pints) of milk,
which is processed immediately after milking. It is
moulded with a ladle twenty-four to twenty-eight hours
after coagulation. It is *cendré* (with vegetable charcoal)
from twenty-four to thirty-six hours after being moulded.
Pougne – the name comes from an ancient location
amalgamated with Hérisson – is eaten fresh (excellent
in spring) or matured. Local people like it quite dry, after
it has ripened for six to eight weeks. Sébastien Gé doesn't
aim for a bluish bloom on the rind; instead he encourages
the growth of a white down (*geotrichum*) that, combined
with the powdered charcoal, gives a greyish colour to the
rind, which tends to form slight ridges. Cheese producers
call this 'curling' and say it is a sign of quality.

Family
Pélardon
Country
France
Area of origin
Gâtine
Animal species
Goat
Milk
Raw
Product
Farmhouse
Optimum ripening
1 month

Rocamadour

France (Midi-Pyrenees)
Goat's milk

This little round disc is covered with a fine, ivory-coloured, slightly velvety growth. It belongs to an illustrious family, the Cabécou – a goat's milk cheese from the south whose origins probably go back to the Arab invasions. In the Languedoc dialect *cabécou* means 'little goat'. Rocamadour gets its name from the magnificent village in the Lot, perched on the side of a cliff. This very popular tourist destination, one of the traditional halts on the road to Santiago di Compostela, rests on a calcareous plateau where the goats browse on vegetation that is very varied and rich in aromatic plants. Rocamadour needs a dozen or so days to ripen. After that its rind tends to give way; if you want to keep it nice and creamy, wrap it and put it in a cool, dry place. But it is far better to eat it as soon as possible, with a light, fragrant, dry white wine – a Sauvignon, perhaps. This is, par excellence, a springtime and summer cheese (the Rocamadour fair is held in June) but it is still delicious right up until autumn. Concentrated pleasure!

Family
Pélardon

Other name
Cabécou de Rocamadour

Country
France

Area of origin
Quercy

Animal species
Goat

Milk
Raw

Product
Farmhouse or cottage industry

Optimum ripening
2 weeks

Rouelle du Tarn
France (Midi-Pyrenees)
Goat's milk

This could be called a goat's milk Murol; with the hole in its centre it is very much like the cheese from Auvergne. But the comparison ends there. Rouelle du Tarn is made from goat's milk by Jeff Rémond, a veteran of the student demonstrations in 1968 and now established on the edge of the Quercy Causses. He started twenty-five years ago with about forty goats and today has five hundred, which are put out to pasture whenever the weather permits – that being any time it is neither raining nor snowing. The rest of the time they are fed cereals and forage made on the farm. Rouelle du Tarn is made by the most typical of farmhouse methods: with raw milk, using lactic ferments (saved from the whey of the day before), and ladle moulded. The major part of the cheeses he produces are *cendré* with organic charcoal; initially black, the rind is made progressively greyer by the formation of a fine yeast-mould (*Geotrichum*). The cheese is about 10 centimetres (4 inches) in diameter and weighs about 250 grams (9 ounces). The central hole is made with a pastry-cutter after 24 hours of drainage in the mould. Jeff, whose products range from Cabécou to a large Tomme weighing two kilos (four and a half pounds), is himself surprised by the success of his Rouelle, which has become a leading product. The idea was suggested to him by my colleague Robert Céneri. His French pun goes: *Il suffit d'un trou pour faire son trou* – all you need is a hole to find your niche!

Family
Pélardon
Autre nom
Rouelle Blanche
Country
France
Area of origin
Tarn
Animal species
Goat
Milk
Raw
Product
Farmhouse
Optimum ripening
1 month

Tomme Capra
France (Rhône-Alpes)
Goat's milk

Family
Pélardon
Country
France
Area of origin
Rhône Valley
Animal species
Goat
Milk
Raw
Product
Farmhouse
Optimum ripening
1 month

This little goat's milk Tomme could be a member of the Picodon family, being similarly close-textured. But it is a little thicker and, more especially, has a more pronounced flavour. A colleague from Vincennes, Bruno Collet, introduced me to it after discovering it in a market near Privas. It is made by a farmer in the village of Saint-Bardou. In order to ease the transport costs (prohibitive for such a small cheese), we recommended it to the wholesale market at Rungis. There are excellent products all over France that would never find outlets outside their local market if they were not offered this 'open Sesame'. Made only with raw milk, Tomme Capra is subject to very careful ripening, for a good month at least. Right from the start the cheeses are selected and assigned as necessary. Some customers require dry cheeses, which need to mature for up to three months and only those Tommes that are not too moist on the surface and have already begun to form a bloom are suitable for this. The cheeses are ventilated at the start of the ripening process (*ressuyage* is the cheesemakers' jargon) to give it an attractive surface. Eventually a fine blue skin appears, not necessary evenly. Like all cheeses of this type, Tomme Capra is at its peak of excellence at the end of spring and the beginning of summer.

Jeff Rémond's Rouelles du Tarn are *cendré* with powdered charcoal straight after unmoulding.

Tomme des Quatres Reines de Forcalquier

France (Provence-Côte d'Azur)
Goat's milk

Family
Pélardon
Country
France
Area of origin
Haute-Provence
Animal species
Goat
Milk
Raw
Product
Farmhouse
Optimum ripening
1 month

There are some flaws in this legend, as told by Frédéric Mistral. The four daughters of the Count of Provence, Raymond de Forcalquier, are said to have married four kings: Louis IX of France, the King of England, the Emperor of Germany and the King of Naples. A likely tale! Two of these 'daughters' belonged to the next generation. But no matter; the story was an inspiration to Charles and Simone Chabot, farmer-cheesemakers and *affineurs* at Valensole, 600 metres (2,000 feet) up in the mountains between Durance and Verdon, not far from Dignes. They have created this very attractive Tomme, adorned with four chestnut leaves and four sprigs of savory – *pèbre d'aï* ('donkey's pepper') in the Occitane dialect – in honour of these four queens. It is basically a Tomme made with two kilos (four and a half pounds) of lactic curd – a process used by many in the region since the 1970s saw the arrival of the 'neo-rural' incomers. It is made from raw milk and shaped in moulds sent from Roquefort. As it ripens – for up to six months to reach its peak – it becomes drier but not more piquant. A good goat-cheese flavour emerges. The rind generally takes on a blue colour after ripening for ten days to a fortnight. Brown or bronze leaves, picked from the trees, are applied to the cheese during the first week.

The Persillé de la Tarentaise family
and related cheeses

The goat's milk cheeses belonging to this family, produced in quite small quantities, are made according to an ancient technique which allows the cheeses to keep longer by heating the curd and then crushing it. Blue appears (or doesn't) in a haphazard manner.

Milk: R = raw, PP = partially pasteurized, P = pasteurized. Product: F = farmhouse, C = cottage industry, I = industrial.

Cheese	Other names	Country/Area of origin	Animal	Milk	Product	Label	Ripening
Bleu de Sainte-Foy		Rhône-Alps	🐄 🐐	R	F		3 months
Persillé de La Clusaz		Northern Savoy	🐄 🐐	R	F		2 months
Persillé de la haute Tarentaise		Haute-Tarentaise	🐐	R	F		3 months
Persillé de la Tarentaise		Savoy – Tarentaise	🐐	R	F		2 months
Persillé de Thônes		Northern Savoy	🐄 🐐	R	F		2 months
Persillé de Tignes	Bleu de Tignes – Tignard	Savoy	🐐	R	F		3 months
Persillé des Aravis		Northern Savoy – Aravis	🐐	R	F		2 months
Persillé du Grand-Bornand		Northern Savoy	🐄 🐐	R	F		2 months
Persillé du Mont-Cenis		Savoy	🐄 🐐	R	F		2 months
Tarentais		Tarentaise	🐐	R	F		1 month

Persillé de la Tarentaise
France (Rhône-Alpes)
Goat's milk

Family
Persillé de la Tarentaise
Country
France
Area of origin
Savoy, Tarentaise
Animal species
Goat
Milk
Raw
Product
Farmhouse
Optimum ripening
2 months

Persillé de la Tarentaise is a rare product made only in the summer, at between 1,800 and 2,000 metres (5,900 and 6,500 feet) on the Val d'Isère road. Rustic in appearance, it comes in the form of a little cylinder, its rind liberally covered with grey, yellow or white mould. On the inside, the cheese seems somewhat coarse and crumbly in parts, showing occasional signs of blue mould. This is a good sign, despite the consumer's apparent preference for white cheeses. Persillé de la Tarentaise owes its characteristics to the unusual way it is made with 're-cooked' curd. The curd is first drained, then kneaded with hot milk before being salted and moulded. Denis Provent, one of the few who know where to find these cheeses, leaves them undisturbed for at least two to three months in a cold cellar. When the quality of the produce allows it, he extends the ripening as far as five months. The number of producers of this little Alpine jewel can be counted on the fingers of one hand, but there is little risk of it disappearing as a family of young cheesemakers has decided to ensure its survival.

Persillé de Tignes

France (Rhône-Alpes)
Goat's milk

This cheese gives me the opportunity, prompted by Denis Provent, to correct a common misconception: a *pâte-persillée* cheese is not a blue-veined cheese, but the product of curd which has been *recuit*, as one used to say in old French – meaning re-cooked. And the 'paste' of this Persillé de Tignes is uniformly white! The recipe for re-cooked curd is a mountain speciality found also in Auvergne: the cheesemaker leaves the curd for a whole day then re-heats it together with a freshly coagulated batch the following day. It is then broken up again and re-moulded. This technique, evolved from practical experience, produces cheeses which keep for much longer. Produced in the Tignes valley and recognizable by its fairly definite flavour, this Persillé was saved from probable extinction by the success of the nearby winter-sports centre. The tourists keep coming back for more and the three or four farmhouse producers have trouble keeping up with demand, while the *affineur* can barely manage to keep the cheeses in his cellars for a month. In the old days they were ripened for six months, at the end of which time blue had developed in the curd.

Family
Persillé de la Tarentaise
Autres noms
Bleu de Tignes, Tignard
Country
France
Area of origin
Savoy
Animal species
Goat
Milk
Raw
Product
Farmhouse
Optimum ripening
3 months

The Pouligny-Saint-Pierre family
and related cheeses

Another way to get noticed! The pyramid is not the most conveniently shaped cheese to cut, but is certainly one of the most attractive.

Milk: R = raw, PP = partially pasteurized, P = pasteurized. Product: F = farmhouse, C = cottage industry, I = industrial.

Cheese	Other names	Country/Area of origin	Animal	Milk	Product	Label	Ripening
Tymsboro		🇬🇧 Avon	🐐	R	F		1 month
Chavroux		🇫🇷	🐐	P	I		1 week
Chef boutonne		🇫🇷 Poitou-Charentes	🐐	R	F, C		1 month
Levroux		🇫🇷 Touraine – Berry	🐐	R, P	I		1 month
Pouligny-saint-pierre	Tour Eiffel	🇫🇷 Indre – Berry	🐐	R	F	AOC-AOP	1 month
Tournon Saint-Martin		🇫🇷 Berry	🐐	R	F		1 month
Valençay	Levroux	🇫🇷 Touraine – Berry	🐐	R	F, I	AOC-AOP	1 month

Pouligny-Saint-Pierre
France (Centre)
Goat's milk

For some obscure reason, the Berry region has given us three goat's milk cheeses shaped like a pyramid, the most famous being this Pouligny-Saint-Pierre, named after a small village in the region. Sometimes called a Tour Eiffel, on account of its pointed shape, its neighbours, Valençay and Levroux – now linked together in the same appellation – are truncated pyramids. This is no mere detail, for the surface-to-weight ratio changes the way in which the cheese ripens and acquires its flavour. I have, generally speaking, a penchant for the Pouligny-Saint-Pierre, as I feel that its texture and taste are more delicate. The moulding, during which great care must be taken not to break up the curd, plays an essential part and is the only way to obtain a very fine-grained cheese. Pouligny is an authentic farmhouse product (small herds still predominate in the Berry region, unlike that of Poitou), and for this reason it is greatly influenced by the changing seasons. I recommend it to you particularly from the month of May, when it is still slightly soft and creamy. A treasure-trove of finesse.

Family
Pouligny-Saint-Pierre
Other name
Tour Eiffel
Country
France
Area of origin
Indre, Berry
Animal species
Goat
Milk
Raw
Product
Farmhouse
Optimum ripening
1 month

Novelty Goat's Milk
and related cheeses

Triangular, heart-shaped, tetrahedron, bell-shaped, or
formed like a drop of water – these cheeses are always
a great hit on the cheeseboard. But it is well worth seeking
out those that have other attractions beside their shape.

Milk: R = raw, PP = partially pasteurized, P = pasteurized. Product: F = farmhouse, C = cottage industry, I = industrial.

Cheese	Other names	Country/Area of origin	Animal	Milk	Product	Label	Ripening
Cabrigan		▋▋ Haute-Provence	🐐	R	F		3 weeks
Chevrion		▋▋ Agenais	🐐	R	F		1 month
Clochette		▋▋ Charente	🐐	R	F		2 weeks
Cœur d'Alvignac		▋▋ Périgord	🐐	R	C		2 weeks
Cœur de chèvre cendré		▋▋ Centre	🐐	R	C		2 weeks
Cœur de Saint-Félix		▋▋ Lauragais	🐐	R	F		3 weeks
Cœur du Berry		▋▋ Berry	🐐	R	C		2 weeks
Cœur Téotski		▋▋ Tarn	🐐	R	F		3 weeks
Goutte		▋▋ Agenais	🐐	R	F		2 weeks
Tétoun		▋▋ Haute-Provence-Plateau de Valensole	🐐	R	F		15 days
Tricorne de Marans		▋▋ Poitou	🐄🐐🐐	R	F		15 days
Trois cornes de Vendée	Sableau – Tribèche – Trébèche	▋▋ Vendée	🐄🐐🐐	R	F		1 month

Coeur Téotski

France (Midi-Pyrenees)
Goat's milk

This little heart-shaped cheese is a real treat, a delicious 'sweetie' to leave melting on the palate. It was invented by a man who took part in the demonstrations of 1968 and came to the Albigeois plateau seeking a different meaning for his life, while nonetheless distancing himself from a certain tradition (that of *Cabécou*). Originally from Macedonia and resident in France for thirty years, Dragan Téotski, the creator of this cheese, spent ten years working in industrial design at Mulhouse before taking up a new trade in the Tarn, birthplace of his wife, Chantal. The farm is about 20 kilometres (12 miles) from Albi, in a hilly, very wooded area – predominantly oak, chestnut and especially hazelnut trees. The acid, shaly soil is not very good for arable farming, but ideal for the hundred or so goats raised on the farm. The cheese is made from raw milk and hand ladled into the moulds. Its delicate, broken white bloom forms naturally. Only 1.5 centimetres (half an inch) thick, it ripens quite quickly, starting from the rind, but care must be taken that the rind remains attached to the curd and doesn't 'wander'. The Coeur Téotski only takes two to three weeks to develop the creamy texture that delights gourmets.

Family
Novelty cheeses
Country
France
Area of origin
Tarn
Animal species
Goat
Milk
Raw
Product
Farmhouse
Optimum ripening
3 weeks

The Maquis Corse family
and related cheeses

Ewe's milk is excellent for making cheeses intended to be eaten fresh. They are often flavoured with herbs and spices.

Milk: R = raw, PP = partially pasteurized, P = pasteurized. Product: F = farmhouse, C = cottage industry, I = industrial.

Cheese	Other names	Country/Area of origin	Animal	Milk	Product	Label	Ripening
Old York		🏴 Yorkshire	🐑	P	C		Fresh
Sussex Slipcote		🏴 Sussex	🐑	R	F		Fresh
Burgos		🇪🇸	🐑	R	C		Fresh
Queso fresco valenciano		🇪🇸	🐑 🐄 🐐 🐑	R	F		Fresh
Villalón	Pata de mulo	🇪🇸	🐑	R, P	C		Fresh
Brebis de Haute-Provence		🇫🇷 Haute-Provence	🐑	R	F		Fresh
Brousse de la Vésubie		🇫🇷 Provence	🐑	R, P	C		Fresh
Caillebotte d'Aunis		🇫🇷 Poitou – Charentes	🐑	R	C		Fresh
Gastanberra		🇫🇷 Basque country	🐑	R,PP	F		Fresh
Jonchée d'Oléron	Oléron	🇫🇷 Aunis	🐑	R	F		Fresh
Maquis Brunelli		🇫🇷 Corsica	🐑	R	F		Fresh
Pigouille		🇫🇷 Île d'Oléron	🐑	R	F		Fresh

The Rove des Garrigues family
and related cheeses

There is a plethora of fresh cheeses made with goat's milk. Unlike ewe's milk, the flavour develops more quickly. They can be eaten just as they are without any enhancement.

Milk: R = raw, PP = partially pasteurized, P = pasteurized. Product: F = farmhouse, C = cottage industry, I = industrial.

Cheese	Other names	Country/Area of origin	Animal	Milk	Product	Label	Ripening
Button	Innes button	Staffordshire	goat	R	C		Fresh
Cerney		Gloucestershire	goat	R	C		Fresh
Perroche		Kent	goat	R	F		Fresh
Galloway goat's milk gems		Dumfries-Galloway	goat	R	F		Fresh
Pant ys gawn		Monmouthshire	goat	P	C		Fresh
Kervella		West	goat	P	F		Fresh
Cabra del tietar		Avila	goat	R	F		Fresh
Flor de oro		Valencia province	cow goat ewe	R	F, C		Fresh
Queso de Murcia		Murcia	goat	R	F, C		Fresh
Besace de pur chèvre		Savoy	goat	R	F		3 weeks
Bouchée de chèvre		Centre	goat	R	C		Fresh
Brousse du Rove		Provence	cow goat ewe	T	F		Fresh
Cabrette du Périgord		Aquitaine	goat	R	C		Fresh
Camisard		Cévennes	goat	R	C		Fresh
Champdenier		Poitou	goat	R	F		Fresh
Pastille de chèvre		Périgord	goat	R	F		Fresh
Petit frais de la ferme		Berry	goat	R	C		Fresh
Rove des garrigues		Languedoc-Roussillon	goat	R	C		Fresh
Cacioricotta		South	goat	R	F		Fresh
Caprini freschi			goat	R	F, C		Fresh

Besace de pur Chèvre

France (Rhône-Alpes)
Goat's milk

Family
Rove des Garrigues
Country
France
Area of origin
Savoy
Animal species
Goat
Milk
Raw
Product
Farmhouse
Optimum ripening
3 weeks

This cheese, with its indeterminate shape, was created by an imaginative farmer in the Tarentaise. It is a 'pre-drained goat's milk cheese', which brings to mind the initial part of the recipe for Mozzarella. After coagulating the milk, the cheesemaker hangs the curd in cloths suspended from the ceiling and leaves it to drain. This is the so-called 'pre-draining' process, an ancient method also used for Tarentais, as well as for Persillé from the Haute Tarentaise. After a certain length of time, the cheesemaker mixes the curd again in a bowl with some hot whey and a little salt, then he energetically squeezes it, just once, in a cloth. A few crafty people, attracted by his success, have tried to copy him, but they were wasting their time! The cloth is removed immediately after the pressing. The shape of the cheese, which weighs about 250 grams (9 ounces), is reminiscent of a shepherd's pouch (a *besace*), which, understandably enough, is the name they gave it. In the course of ripening (three to four weeks at the most), a fine, whitish rind forms, as light as that of the Saint-Marcellin. The finest feature of this Besace is its softness on the palate.

Brousse du Rove

France (Provence-Côte d'Azur)
Goat's, cow's or ewe's milk

Brousse du Rove is sold in a strange, elongated plastic mould – sometimes charmingly called a 'fairy's finger'. It would collapse disastrously if removed from it. This mould is based on the shape of the ram's horn which was used in earlier times and subsequently replaced by tubes made of tin-plate or plaited rushes. Brousse was first made, a very long time ago, in the regions inland from Marseilles, where there have always been goats of the Rove breed. Nowadays, ewe's milk and even cow's milk are used by the three remaining farmers still in production. The recipe consumes a great deal of energy; immediately after milking the milk is heated to 80°C (175°F) then acidified with white vinegar, or acetic acid, to curdle it. The cheesemaker then beats it vigorously with a whisk (*brousser* means 'to whisk') until it forms globules. These are collected with a skimmer and placed in the moulds, where they agglomerate and settle. The process is similar to that used in the making of *Brocciu* with the difference that *Brocciu* uses whey rather than full milk. All that remains to be done is to 'decant' the Brousse onto a plate and enjoy it. Its acidic flavour needs some kind of sweet accompaniment, such as a red fruit coulis, honey, sugar and – why not – a few drops of strong alcohol. A true dessert cheese!

Family
Rove des Garrigues
Country
France
Area of origin
Provence
Animal species
Cow, goat or ewe
Milk
Partially pasteurized
Product
Farmhouse
Optimum ripening
Fresh

The cottage cheese family

Cow's milk is made into a whole range of more or less fat-free cheeses for eating fresh. They are sometimes extended with cream or crème fraîche or mixed with herbs and spices of all kinds.

Milk: R = raw, PP = partially pasteurized, P = pasteurized. Product: F = farmhouse, C = cottage industry, I = industrial.

Cheese	Other names	Country/Area of origin	Animal	Milk	Product	Label	Ripening
Dopplerahmfrischkäse			🐄	P	I		Fresh
Körniger frischkäse			🐄	P	I		Fresh
Quark	Speisequark	Bavaria	🐄	P	C, I		Fresh
Rahmfrischkäse			🐄	P	I		Fresh
Schitkäse			🐄	P	I		Fresh
Cambridge			🐄	PP, P	I		Fresh
Colwick cheese			🐄	P	I		Fresh
Cornish pepper		Cornwall	🐄	P	C		Fresh
Lactic cheese			🐄	P	I		Fresh
Paneer			🐄	P	I		Fresh
Single cream cheese			🐄	P	I		Fresh
York			🐄	PP, P	I		Fresh
Kugelkäse		Danube	🐄	R	C		Fresh
Sauerkäse			🐄	P	C, I		Fresh
Topfen			🐄	P	I		Fresh
Caboc		Ross-Cromarty	🐄	P	C		Fresh
Crowdie		Ross-Cromarty	🐄	P	F		Fresh
Afuega'l Pitu		Asturias	🐄	R	F		Fresh
Cream Cheese			🐄	P	I		Fresh
Aligot	Tomme fraîche de l'Aubrac	Midi-Pyrenees-Rouergue-Auvergne	🐄	R, P	F, C, I		Fresh
Bibbelkäse		Alsace	🐄	P	C		Fresh
Boulamour			🐄	R	C		Fresh
Boursin		Normandy	🐄	P	I		Fresh
Cailles rennaises		Brittany	🐄	R, P	C		Fresh
Carré frais			🐄	P	I		Fresh
Cervelle de canut	Claqueret lyonnais	Lyons region	🐄	P	C, I		Fresh
Chèvre frais du Berry		Berry	🐄	R	F		Fresh

Cheese	Other names	Country/Area of origin	Animal	Milk	Product	Label	Ripening
Coulandon		Bourbonnais		R	C		Fresh
Crémet nantais		Nantes region		R, P	F, C, I		Fresh
Demi-sel		Bray region		P	I		Fresh
Fontainebleau		Île-de-France		R, P	C		Fresh
Fromage à la pie		West		R, P	I		Fresh
Gournay frais	Malakoff	Normandy		P	C		Fresh
Jonchée niortaise		Poitou		R	F		Fresh
Petit suisse				P	I		Fresh
Poustagnac		Guyenne		R	C		Fresh
Saint-florentin		Auxerrois		P	C, I		Fresh
Saint-Moret				P	I		Fresh
Samos				P	I		Fresh
Ségalou		Quercy		R	F		Fresh
Tartare				P	I		Fresh
Quark				P	C, I		Fresh
Bresso				R	C		Fresh
Crescenza		Lombardy		P	C, I		Fresh
Giuncata		Southern Italy		R, P	C, I		Fresh
Graukäse		Tirol		R, P	C		Fresh
Mascarpone		Lombardy		P	C, I		Fresh
Murazzano		Piedmont		R	C, I	AOC-AOP	Fresh
Pannarello		Veneto-Friuli		P	C, I		Fresh
Prescinseûa		Genoa		P	C, I		Fresh
Raviggiolo		Emilia-Romagna		R, P	C, I		Fresh
Squacquerone		Emilia-Romagna		P	C, I		Fresh
Stracchino		Lombardy		P	I		Fresh
Cottage cheese		Universal		R, PP, P	C, I		Fresh
Fromage blanc		Universal		R, PP, P	F, C, I		Fresh
Fromage frais		Universal		R, PP, P	C, I		Fresh

Boulamour

France

Cow's milk

This most original cheese has already travelled all around the world. It was created by Adèle Forteau, my predecessor at Rue de Grenelle, in Paris. When I took over here in 1971, my wife Nicole developed the recipe further by perfecting the basic principles. She starts by macerating sultanas and currants in kirsch for one month then, when they are thoroughly impregnated with the alcohol, she mixes them into a triple-cream cheese from Burgundy to which she adds a little extra salt. Everything is done by hand; the texture has to be fairly malleable to lend itself to this treatment. The result is an astonishing dessert cheese, which combines the sweet flavours of the fruit with the salty taste of the cheese, the whole titillated by the alcohol. Boulamour has been most successful across the Atlantic, where it even has its imitators, largely because of its name. Marilyn Monroe was infatuated by the word *amour* and the sensuous way she pronounced it gave it such a cachet in the Anglo-Saxon countries that the ground was already laid for Boulamour. I recommend it at aperitif time, with a glass of champagne.

Family
Cottage Cheese
Country
France
Area of origin
Savoy
Animal species
Cow
Milk
Raw
Product
Cottage industry
Optimum ripening
Fresh

Cervelle de Canut

France (Rhône-Alpes)
Cow's milk

Cervelle de Canut occupies a prominent place on the café menus in Lyons. It is a fresh white cheese copiously seasoned with different herbs and flavourings: chives, garlic, shallot, parsley, chervil. One can also add fresh whipped cream to give it more volume and delicacy. Everyone has a personal version. This cheese is generally eaten, nicely chilled, at the end of a meal. An absolute delight on the terraces of Lyons at lunchtime, when the sun is raising the temperature in the Rhône valley. Cervelle de Canut is closely linked with the history of the Lyons – the 'silk town'. It was, it seems, a great favourite with the *canuts*, the workers charged with silk weaving. As for the term *cervelle* (brain), the modern cheese manifests little resemblance to our grey matter, but no doubt it had a rougher, less regular texture in those days. A very local product which it is quite possible to make at home, it is rarely sold anywhere except Lyons, usually in the central markets, where each retailer extols his own particular version.

Family
Cottage cheese
Autre nom
Claqueret Lyonnais
Country
France
Area of origin
Lyons region
Animal species
Cow
Milk
Pasteurized
Product
Cottage industry
or industrial
Optimum ripening
Fresh

Jonchée Niortaise

France (Poitou-Charentes)
Cow's milk

Jonchée is a traditional product of the marshes on the Atlantic coast. Its distinctive feature is its natural organic wrapping – made from a plant that grows freely in the area – which give is its irregular, elongated appearance. It is sold very fresh. Éric Jarnan, who recently took over from his parents and is one of only four cheesemakers producing it, sells it on the day it is made. He coagulates the raw milk (one litre (1.8 pints) makes about two and a half Joncs) very early in the morning. In the old days it was curdled using a species of blue-flowered thistle, similar to a small artichoke, but coagulation using rennet takes only 20 minutes. Once set, the curd is ladled onto little mats made of green rushes, run up on a sewing machine, which are rolled and tied at both ends. They are then ready to eat and Éric loads them onto his van and delivers some to various markets before making the rounds of his customers door to door. Those not sold that day are thrown away. The rushes, collected all year round, are picked green and supple, neither too thick nor too thin. A special characteristic of the cheese is the flavour of the few drops of bitter almond extract Éric adds to the milk. The rushes themselves give no particular flavour to the cheese.

Family
Cottage cheese
Country
France
Area of origin
Poitou
Animal species
Cow
Milk
Raw
Product
Farmhouse
Optimum ripening
Fresh

Jonchée Niortaise are wrapped in aquatic sedge leaves. A product with a very short life, it is best eaten on the day it is made.

The Gardian family
and related cheeses

In areas where a great deal of stock is raised, milks from different animal species are traditionally used together or alternated according to the various lactation cycles. This results in cheeses that frequently change their appearance.

Milk: R = raw, PP = partially pasteurized, P = pasteurized. Product: F = farmhouse, C = cottage industry, I = industrial.

Cheese	Other names	Country/Area of origin	Animal	Milk	Product	Label	Ripening
Cádiz		Andalucia		R, P	C		Fresh
Cervera		South		R, P	C		Fresh
Cuajada				R P	F, C		Fresh
Málaga		Andalucia		R, P	C		Fresh
Mato		Catalonia		R	F		Fresh
Puzol		South		R, P	C		Fresh
Juustoleipä				P	F, C, I		Fresh
Munajuusto	Ilves			P	F, C, I		Fresh
Caillebotte	Jonchée	Poitou-Charentes		R	F, C, I		Fresh
Gardian		Provence		R, P	F, C, I		Fresh
Feta				R, PP, P	I		Fresh
Caciotta		Centre		R	F, C		Fresh
Robiola		Piedmont-Lombardy		R, P	F, C, I		Fresh
Robiola di roccaverano		Piedmont		R	F, C	AOC-AOP	Fresh

Gardian

France (Provence-Côte d'Azur)
Goat's milk

Christian Fleury belongs to the 'neo-rural' generation;
he acquired his first goats in 1968. Since 1976 he has
been based on the plain of Comtat Venaisson, near
Saint-Rémy-de-Provence, outside Arles. He keeps a herd
of fifty or so goats, which are fed essentially on the excellent
hay from the neighbouring plain of Crau. In particular he
makes a small Tomme Fraîche called Le Gardian, which I
strongly recommend. This very mild cheese is topped with
a bay leaf and sprinkled with fennel seeds, pepper and often
a few aniseed grains too. Not forgetting a drizzle of olive oil.
Very fresh on the palate, it is typical of a cheese that should
be eaten at the start of a meal rather than at the end. If you
want to eat it at the end anyway, I suggest you have it as a
dessert, with a touch of something sweet, like honey.
Gardian is sold the day it is made. It also comes in a ripened
version which, after three weeks, has an unctuous, almost
creamy texture. That is the one they prefer in the area
around Arles. At one time, when the Mistral blew, the
cheese had a tendency to dry out. In the farmhouses it
was moistened with white wine or eau-de-vie then put to
macerate in an earthenware jar so as not to put a strain on
the jaws!

Family
Cottage cheese
Country
France
Area of origin
Provence
Animal species
Goat
Milk
Raw or pasteurized
Product
Farmhouse, cottage
industry or industrial
Optimum ripening
Fresh

The Provolone family
and related cheeses

The 'drawn-curd' technique – a great Italian speciality –
produces cheeses that, if left to ripen for long enough
(up to two or three years!), develop a very dry curd which
can be smoked. They are used primarily in cooking

Milk: R = raw, PP = partially pasteurized, P = pasteurized. Product: F = farmhouse, C = cottage industry, I = industrial.

Cheese	Other names	Country/Area of origin	Animal	Milk	Product	Label	Ripening
Pastorello		Victoria		P	I		6 months
Provolone American				P	I		6 months
Kasseri	Kaseri			R	C, I	AOC-AOP	3 months
Caciocavallo		Southern Italy		R, P	F, C, I		1 year
Caciocavallo silano		Southern Italy		R, P	F, C, I	AOC-AOP	1 year
Provolone		Lombardy		R, P	I		6 months
Provolone del monaco		Campagna		R	C		1 year
Provolone valdapana		Northern Italy		P	C, I	AOC-AOP	1 year
Ragusano		Sicily		R	C	AOC-AOP	6 months

Imposing Provolone cheeses hanging in the cellars
of the Guffanti Company, at Arona. One cheese
can weigh as much as 100 kilos (220 pounds) and
needs a year to come to maturity. Provolone is
mainly used in cooking.

The Mozzarella family
and related cheeses

The 'drawn-curd' cheeses made with cow's or buffalo's milk are very acidic and fill the mouth with an intense freshness. These very malleable cheeses can be made in any shape the imagination can come up with.

Milk: R = raw, PP = partially pasteurized, P = pasteurized. Product: F = farmhouse, C = cottage industry, I = industrial.

Cheese	Other names	Country/Area of origin	Animal	Milk	Product	Label	Ripening
Haloumi			🐄🐐🐑	R,PP, P	C, I		Fresh
Bocconcini		All Italy	🐄	P	I		Fresh
Burrata		Apuglia	🐄	R	F, C		Fresh
Burrata di Andria			🐄	R	F, C		Fresh
Burrino	Butirro, burri	Southern Italy	🐄	R, P	F, C, I		1 month
Fior di latte	Mozzarella di vacca	Campagna-Latium	🐄🐃	R, P	C, I		Fresh
Mozzarella di bufala campana		Latium-Campagna	🐃	R	C, I	AOC-AOP	Fresh
Scamorza		Southern Italy	🐄	R, P	F, C		1 week
Vastedda del belice		Sicily	🐑	R, P	F, C		Fresh

The Brocciu family
and related cheeses

Using the whey left from the production of one cheese to make
another, different form of cheese is a universal practice. It results
in a variety of cheeses, which are sometimes enriched with cream,
or flavoured with herbs or spices to give them more character.

Milk: R = raw, PP = partially pasteurized, P = pasteurized. Product: F = farmhouse, C = cottage industry, I = industrial.

Cheese	Other names	Country/Area of origin	Animal	Milk	Product	Label	Ripening
Requeson				R	I		Fresh
Brebis frais du Caussedou		Quercy		R	F		Fresh
Breuil	Cenberona	Basque country		R	F		Fresh
Brocciu	Broccio – Brucciu	Corsica		R, PP, P	F	AOC-AOP	Fresh
Gaperon	Gapron	Auvergne		R, P	F, C		2 months
Greuilh	Zembera	Pyrenees		R	F		Fresh
Sérac	Recuite	Savoy		R	F		Fresh
Anthotyro				R	F, C		Fresh
Manouri		Crete – Macedonia		R	F, C	AOC-AOP	Fresh
Myzithra	Mitzithra			R	F, C		Fresh
Xynotyro				R	F, C		Fresh
Ricotta di pecora				R, P	F, C, I		Fresh
Ricotta piacentina				R, P	F, C, I		Fresh
Ricotta romana				R, P	F, C, I		Fresh
Seirass		Piedmont		R	F, C		Fresh
Seirass del Fieno		Piedmont		R	F, C		Fresh
Requeijão				R	I		Fresh
Mesost				P	I		2 weeks
Zieger	Ziger	German Switzerland		R, P	C		Fresh

Gaperon

France (Auvergne)
Buttermilk and cow's milk whey

Family
Brocciu
Other name
Gapron
Country
France
Area of origin
Auvergne
Animal species
Cow
Milk
Raw or pasteurized
Product
Farmhouse or
cottage industry
Optimum ripening
2 months

No part of the milk is wasted. After the cheese is made, the remaining whey can be used to feed pigs or calves, or made into another, less calorific form of cheese (Ricotta or Cancoillotte, for example). The buttermilk left after churning butter can also be made into cheese. Gaperon, a product that originated in Limagne, is one of these. This white, dome-shaped cheese is made from *gaspe* or *gape* which is Auvergne *patois* for buttermilk. To give it a little flavour the peasants used to add salt, pepper and, above all, garlic (Billom, in Auvergne, is the garlic capital). The ingredients are chopped and added to the buttermilk, and if necessary, a little curdled cow's milk and some whey is added. The whole cheese, after being carefully kneaded and drained in a large cloth, is hung from the ceiling or near the fireplace, where it takes on a smoky flavour. Gaperon can then be ripened on rye straw. In days gone by, the amount of cheeses thus produced was considered to be an outward indication of wealth, and was taken into consideration when discussing a young girl's dowry. Today, Gaperon is enriched and its texture is not so dry, but the flavour is still very pronounced.

In their little wooden boxes the wrinkled Gaperons wait patiently to make their appearance on the cheese merchants' shelves.

The Cancoillotte family
and related cheeses

These melted cheeses are a by-product of cheese making. The majority of them are made from cheeses either left over, or damaged in production, broken up and melted together.

Milk: R = raw, PP = partially pasteurized, P = pasteurized. Product: F = farmhouse, C = cottage industry, I = industrial.

Cheese	Other names	Country/Area of origin	Animal	Milk	Product	Label	Ripening
Abgesottener käse			🐄	P	I		Fresh
Glundner käse			🐄	P	I		Fresh
Kochkäse			🐄	P	I		Fresh
Kacheke's			🐄	P	I		Fresh
Cook cheese			🐄	P	I		Fresh
Cancoillotte	Colle	Franche-Comté	🐄	R, PP, P	C, I		Fresh
Rambol		Yvelines	🐄	P	I		Fresh
Vache qui Rit		Franche-Comté	🐄	P	I		Fresh
Smeltkaas			🐄	P	C, I		2 months
Fjäll Brynt			🐄	P	I		Fresh
Crème de gruyère			🐄	P	C		Fresh

The strong cheese family
and related cheeses

No longer in favour with many people, these strong cheeses were the everyday fare of generations of peasants who preserved them in sealed containers with alcohol and spices – both used for their antiseptic properties.

Milk: R = raw, PP = partially pasteurized, P = pasteurized. Product: F = farmhouse, C = cottage industry, I = industrial.

Cheese	Other names	Country/Area of origin	Animal	Milk	Product	Label	Ripening
Cabécou des mineurs		Aveyron – Decazeville region		R	F		1 month
Cachaille		Provence		R	C		3 months
Cachat	Fromage fort du mont Ventoux	Provence		R,PP	C		1 month
Confit d'époisses		Burgundy		R,PP	C		1 month
Foudjou		Auvergne		R, P	C		3 months
Fremgeye		Lorraine		R, P	C		3 months
Fromage en pot		Lorraine		R, P	C		3 months
Fromage fort de Lens		Nord		R	C		3 months
Fromage fort du Lyonnais		Lyons region		R, P	C		2 months
Fromagée du Larzac		Larzac		P	C, I		3 months
Pâte de fromage		Northern Corsica		R	F, C		6 months
Pâtefine fort		Dauphiné		R	C		3 months
Pétafine		Lyons region		R	C		1 month
Pitchou		Dauphiné		P	C		2 months
Trang'nat	Gueyin	Lorraine		R, P	C		3 months
Bruss		Piedmont		R, P	C		4 months
Ricotto forte		Apuglia		P	C		3 months

Pétafine

France (Rhône-Alpes)
Cow's milk whey

Family
Strong cheeses
Country
France
Area of origin
Lyons region
Animal species
Cow
Milk
Raw
Product
Cottage industry
Optimum ripening
1 month

In the Lyons region they have a veritable passion for gastronomy in liquid form; wine, of course – the Rhône valley is richly endowed with that – and also cheeses that lend themselves to ripening to a very creamy, runny consistency that can be easily spread on bread. On the western slopes of the valley one finds different sorts of Brique, including Brique du Forez; on the eastern slopes there is Saint-Marcellin, which *La Mère Richard* made fashionable in the markets of Lyons, ancient capital of Roman Gaul. Pétafine is in the same category; it also recaptures another Lyons tradition, that of macerated cheeses. It is made to an old local domestic recipe for a cheese made from whey – *pâte fine* (fine paste), which became Pétafine. The local cooks used to mix raisins and leftover grated cheese into this little whey cheese and put it to macerate in the local 'gut-rot' alcohol. The result, formed into a ball and rolled in breadcrumbs, had a light brown curd, which was spread on stale bread or toast to accompany the house wine. This is one of the things cheese was used for in Lyons – to make people thirsty. I used to deliver Pétafines to the Élysée Palace when Georges Pompidou was President of the Republic. He was very fond of them. The hygiene regulations have now put an end to the marketing of this 'shepherd's pie of the cheese world' and it only survives in domestic kitchens. It should, naturally, be accompanied by a strong alcohol in order to remain in character.

The Boulette family
and related cheeses

Generally eaten very fresh, Boulettes are a great speciality in northern France. They are fairly low-fat cheeses, kneaded with herbs and spices.

Milk: R = raw, PP = partially pasteurized, P = pasteurized. Product: F = farmhouse, C = cottage industry, I = industrial.

Cheese	Other names	Country/Area of origin	Animal	Milk	Product	Label	Ripening
Boulette de Charleroi		🇧🇪	🐄	P	C		Fresh
Boulette de Namur		🇧🇪	🐄	P	C		Fresh
Boulette de Romedenne		🇧🇪	🐄	P	C		Fresh
Boulette d'Avesnes		🇫🇷 Avesnois (Flanders)	🐄	R, P	F, C, I		3 months
Boulette de Cambrai		🇫🇷 Cambrésis	🐄	R, P	F, C		Fresh
Boulette des moines		🇫🇷 Burgundy	🐄	R	C		Fresh

Industrially made cheeses
An inescapable modern phenomenon

Products of pasteurization and marketing, modern industrial products do not pretend to be gastronomic cheeses. Produced on a vast scale and destined mainly for multiple outlets, their flavour is constant and reliable for consumption throughout the year. Their popularity is heavily dependent on major television advertising campaigns. In France, the two main specialist manufacturers are the Bongrain group and the Bel cheese company. These are some of the best-known ones.

Babybel
Modelled on the Dutch Edam, Babybel was created in 1931. Its compact size and its red wax protective shell make it ideal for snacks and picnics.

Belle des Champs
Made from cow's milk, this bloomy-rind, soft-pressed cheese has a very mild flavour and an extremely supple texture.

Boursin
Backed by a catchy, rhyming advertising slogan that became a cult – *du vin, du pain, du Boursin* (some wine, some bread, some Boursin,) – this little fresh cheese, flavoured with garlic and fresh herbs, was created in 1963. Soft and creamy, it is made in Normandy from cow's milk. Enriched with cream, and with no rind, it is also made in pepper, chive or walnut versions.

Bresse Bleu
Modelled on Gorgonzola, this blue cheese came into being in the Bresse region just after the Second World War. Made from cow's milk, it is made to be eaten creamy.

Caprice des Dieux
Eaten in 150 countries, this bloomy-rind, lozenge-shaped cheese was created at Illoud-en-Bassigny, in the Northern Marne region in 1956, by Jean-Noël Bongrain. Made from cow's milk, it is notable for its creamy texture.

Chaumes
Launched in 1972, this cheese was modelled on Munster and is very similar to it in appearance. Its flavour, however, is much milder – more like the Trappiste cheeses. It is made in the south-west of France. Initially it was cut and served by weight from supermarket cheese counters.

Chavroux

Created in 1985, this truncated-pyramid shaped fresh cheese is made from goat's milk.
It leaves a great impression of freshness on the palate.

Étorki

A copy of the traditional Pyrenean ewe's milk cheeses, this one is made in the Basque country.
Not too strongly flavoured, it has a firm curd and an almost creamy texture.

Kiri

This 'cheese for gourmets in short trousers' was first made in 1968. It is a fresh cheese, melted
and blended with cream and intended for sandwiches.

Leerdamer

A Dutch version of Swiss Emmenthal, the flavour of Leerdamer is fruitier but less intense. Its
curd is quite supple.

Port Salut

Heir to the cheeses made by the monks of the Abbey at Entrammes in 1816, Port Salut is the
most famous of the Trappiste cheeses. It is very mild, with a smooth texture.

Rouy

Created at the beginning of the last century in Burgundy, it was modelled on Pont-l'Évêque.
Beneath its streaked orange rind its paste has all the delicate aromas of cow's milk.

Saint-Albray

First made in the Béarn region in 1977, this cheese is easily recognized by its unusual shape –
like a flower with six petals. The curd is soft and creamy beneath the orange rind with its fine
white bloom.

Tartare

Like Boursin – the cheese it was created to compete with – Tartare is made in several versions:
garlic and fresh herbs, walnut, three peppers, etc. It is particularly good on toast.

Vache qui Rit

Launched by Léon Bel in 1921, Vache qui Rit is now recognized all over the world. Originally
it was a melted cheese made with broken pieces of Gruyère.

RIPENING • DOUBLE CREAM • CURD • PASTEURIZATION • SALINE SOLUTION • CURDLING • APPELLATION OF ORIGIN

Appendix
The vocabulary of the cheese world

The vocabulary of the cheese world

Affinage (cheese-ripening): the process of bringing a cheese to the phase of maturity when it reaches its optimum flavour.

Appellation d'origine controlée (AOC) (Appellation of Origin Controlled): appellation that defines and protects those products having a strict link to a specific area.

Appellation d'origine protegée (AOP) (Appellation of Origin Protected): a European Union version of AOC.

Bloom: mould which develops on the surface of a cheese. It may be white, yellow, red, blue, etc., and distributed over the rind evenly or in patches.

Bloomy rind: rind covered with a white mould.

Brushed rind: often greyish rind which has been brushed during ripening to remove excessive moulds.

Buron: name given in Auvergne to a small workplace in the mountains where cheeses are made and ripened in the summer.

Buttermilk: whitish liquid left over after butter is churned.

Casein: the main protein contained in milk. The richer the milk the better it is for cheese making.

Cayolar (or etchola): a Basque word for a mountain workplace where ewe's milk Tommes are made in the summer.

Coagulation: the action of curdling which causes the milk proteins to agglomerate.

Cujala: a mountain workplace in the Béarn region, where ewe's milk Tommes are made during the summer.

Curd: coagulated milk.

Curd made with rennet (or sweet curd): milk coagulated mainly using rennet. This method is fairly fast and gives a quite firm curd.

Curd-cutter: implement used to cut curd into small pieces to help the whey drain from it.

Curdling: transforming milk into a solid form by coagulation.

Dairy: the opposite of 'farmhouse'; it applies to cheeses made from milk collected from several dairy farms.

Double Cream: a cheese enriched with fresh cream with at least a 60 per cent fat content (i.e. 60 per cent of the total solids without the water content).

Drawn paste: paste in which the curd forms strings when stretched, after being boiled several times.

Dry extract: that which would be left if the water content of the cheese were removed. The fat-content figure quoted on the label is a percentage of this and not of the actual cheese.

Estive: the summer period when the animals are taken to the high mountain pastures. The cheeses are made in situ during this time.

Etchola: see Cavolar.

Farmhouse: said of a cheese made by a single commercial concern from milk also produced by it.

Ferment: the catch-all term that includes bacteria (including lactic bacteria), fungi (including the various species of mould), and yeasts.

Fermentation: process by which the milk turns to cheese under the action of various micro-organisms.

Fissure: a crack that can appear in hard cheeses. This is not a flaw but a natural phenomenon.

Fruitière: name given to cheese dairies in the Alpine regions, to which farmers take their milk to be made into cheese.

Hâloir: a drying room where the cheeses are placed immediately after they are made.

IGP – Indication géographique protégée (Protected geographical area): European appellation defining and protecting products that have the advantage of belonging to a specific area.

Jasserie: a mountain workshop where cheeses are made in the Forez region.

Lactic curd: milk coagulated mainly by the use of lactic ferments. It is quite acidic. This method of coagulation is fairly slow and the curds take some time to drain.

Lactic ferments: ferments that feed on the milk sugars (lactose), producing lactic acid in the process.

Lactose: milk sugar.

Morge: French word referring to the viscous substance that gradually forms on the surface of firm cheeses that are washed during ripening.

Mould: a microscopic fungus that can develop on the rind of cheeses or in the curd itself. The best known of these are the penicilliums.

Pasteurization: process of heating milk to a temperature between 75 and 90°C (167 and 194°F) for a few seconds, thus eliminating the major part of the micro-organisms it contained.

Penicillium: a family of moulds.

Raw milk: milk direct from the udders (at approximately 37°C (99°F)) which has not been heated above 40°C (104°F).

Rennet: digestive enzyme taken from the fourth stomach of young ruminants (this makes cheese a pre-digested product). Nowadays there are synthetic forms of rennet.

Rennet coagulation: 'setting' the milk by adding rennet to make it solidify.

Rennet stomach: the abomasum, or lining of the fourth stomach of a young ruminant, used in the production of traditional rennet.

Report: French word meaning roughly 'transfer' – used to describe a change in the way a food-stuff is consumed: e.g. milk, which is liquid, becomes cheese – a solid.

Rocou: an orange colouring obtained from the seeds of the tropical annatto – a tree of the *bixaceae* family.

Saumure: water saturated with salt.

Sedge: strips of the leaves of these water reeds are used to bind Livarot cheeses. Paper strips are now largely used in their place.

Seeding: the addition of ferments or moulds either to the milk, the curd or the rind.

Thermization: a lesser form of pasteurization during which the milk is heated to between 63° and 68°C (145 and 154°F) for a few seconds up to a few minutes.

Triple cream: fresh cheese enriched with fresh cream of which the solid matter is made up of at least 75 per cent fat content.

Washed rind: a damp rind, orange-ish in colour, with a strong smell resulting from repeated washing with salt water in the ripening process.

Whey (a 5 per cent solution of lactose in water): watery liquid left after the curd has been drained.

Index

In this index the cheeses are shown in alphabetical order. Page numbers in **bold** indicate the tables of cheese families; those in *italics* indicater the 'favourites'.

Acknowledgements. The authors would like to thank all those who contributed to this book by their advice, help and availability: Philippe Abrahamse, Yves Adrian, Nicole Aigoin, Jean-Charles Arnaud, Noël Autexier, Louis-Marie Barreau, Alain Barthélemy, Patrick Beaumont, Jean Berthaut, Frank Bertrand, M. Biet, Sylvie Boubrit, Daniel Boujon, Eric Bourges, Frédéric Brand, Madeleine and Jean-François Brunelli, José Luis Ordonnez Casal, Caseificio Rossi, Charles and Simone Chabot, Thierry Chévenet, Christiana Clerici, Bruno Collet, Consortium Parmigiano Reggiano, Daniel Delahaye, Domaine de Deves Nouvel, Jean-François and Rosine Dombre, Gilles Dubois, Michel Dubois, Jacques-Alain Dufaux, Jean and Peyo Etcheleku, Carlo Fiori, Christian Fleury, Philippe Garros, Bernard Gaud, Sébastien Gê, Claudine Gillet, André Girard, Gilles and Odile Goursat, Thierry Graindorge, Fromagerie Guiguet, La Graine Johé Didier Jean, Gérard Gratiot, Claire Guillemette, Dominique Guzman, Virginie and Jacques Haxaire, Alain Hess, Eric Jarnan, Philippe Jaubert, Joe Joffre, Gérard Leclère, Claude Leduc, Christian Le Gall, Magali Legras, Jean-Claude Le Jaouen, Claude Leroux, Luc Lesénécal, M. and Mme Hervé Loussouarn, Juan Manuel Martinez Mora, Claudine Mayer, Philippe Meslon, Maryse Micheaud, Christian Moyersoen, Philippe Olivier, Joseph Paccard, Frère Paul, Marthe Pégourié, Roland Perrin, Denis Provent, Jean Puig, Baptiste Raynal, Jeff Rémond, Claudia and Wolfgang Reuss, Patricia Ribier, Olivier Richard, Jean Salat, René Schertenleib, Simone and Rémi Seguin, Isabelle Seignemartin, Hélène Servant, M. Sigonneau, Dragan and Chantal Téotski, André Valadier, Rudi and Helen Vehren, M. Vermot, M. Veyrat, Claudine Vigier. **Roland Barthélemy** would particularly like to thank Nicole and Claire, as well as the whole team at Rue de Grenelle, Michel Rougeault and all the members of the Guide des Fromagers, and of course his friends. Without them this book would not have been possible. **Arnaud Sperat-Czar** would particularly like to thank Anne-Sibylle Loiseau, his colleagues at 'L'Amateur de Fromage', Alexandre Espoir-Duroy, Jean Garsuault, Joseph Hossenlop, Loïc Kerjean, Serge Michels, Hubert Richard and François Sperat-Czar, as well as Caroline and Joséphine for their care and infinite patience. **Daniel Czap** extends his thanks to Marie-Line Salaün for her efficiency, 'Madame est servie' for their invaluable help with transport and, of course, Roland Barthélemy for his ready availability.